LIFE WORLD LIBRARY

IRELAND

LIFE WORLD LIBRARY

IRELAND

by Joe McCarthy
and The Editors of LIFE

TIME-LIFE INTERNATIONAL (Nederland) N.V.

COVER: A man from the Aran
Island of Inishmore rests
beside a stone wall which runs
along the cliffs
overlooking the sea.

ABOUT THE WRITER

Joe McCarthy, author of the interpretive text for this volume of the LIFE World Library, is an American writer and editor of Irish extraction. His father was a native of County Kerry, his mother of County Kilkenny. Mr. McCarthy was born in Cambridge, Massachusetts. He was educated at Boston College, and worked before World War II as a reporter and sports-writer on the now-defunct Boston *Post*. During the war he served first with the U.S. Army artillery and then became sports editor, war correspondent and managing editor of *Yank*, the American Army weekly, attaining the rank of master sergeant. Since the war, Mr. McCarthy has been a frequent contributor to American publications. His best-known book is *The Remarkable Kennedys*, a perceptive account of the Kennedy family published in Great Britain in 1962. Mr. McCarthy is also the author of a number of articles on Ireland for American magazines. He travelled extensively through the island in 1962 and again in 1963.

Contents

TIME/LIFE BOOKS

EDITOR
Norman P. Ross

TEXT DIRECTOR   ART DIRECTOR
William Jay Gold   Edward A. Hamilton

CHIEF OF RESEARCH
Beatrice T. Dobie

EDITORIAL STAFF FOR "IRELAND"

EDITOR, LIFE WORLD LIBRARY   *Oliver E. Allen*
DESIGNER   *Ben Schultz*
CHIEF RESEARCHER   *Grace Brynolson*

The text for this book was written by Joe McCarthy, the picture essays by David S. Thomson and Edmund V. White. Many of the photographs were taken by Brian Seed. The following individuals and departments of Time Inc. were helpful in producing the book: Carl Mydans, LIFE staff photographer; Doris O'Neil, Chief, LIFE Picture Library; Philip Payne and Katharine Sachs, TIME-LIFE News Service; and Content Peckham, Chief, Bureau of Editorial Reference. This international edition adapted by Laura Ford.

Introduction

It is appropriate that the LIFE World Library series on the nations of the world should devote a full volume to the Irish. Americans' affinities with both the North and South of Ireland are numerous. Many of us are Irish. Many more of us have a sympathy with Ireland defined by history and religion and the mutual experience of life on the perimeters of the North Atlantic. We can rejoice in the good signs that the myriad sufferings and frustrations of Irishmen in their beautiful yet stormy island lie in the past.

As Mr. McCarthy's narrative indicates, the bitterness generated by civil wars has receded. With Irish independence largely a reality, Irishmen are proving to be among the sanest of self-governors. In this decade they have also achieved the extra energy and balance and wisdom to be a force for reason out of all proportion to their numbers. In the General Assembly, in U.N. peace-keeping operations in the Congo, in their counsel to less developed countries, their presence as a nation is freedom's good fortune. Just as the Irish and their descendants scattered through the world have in the main been the most responsible of individuals, so the Irish nation now can and does act as a responsible element in a world in which that element is all too scarce.

Trinity College and the National University of Ireland colleges in Dublin, Cork and Galway educate many hundreds of students from the world's under-developed, newer nations. Indeed, at least two ministers of the Government and several of the other leaders of Nigeria, one of the important new African nations, have led a university life in Dublin. Although Ireland left the British Commonwealth in 1949, its Government in preceding years of association did much to define the greater flexibility of Commonwealth membership which today still binds Britain to many of its former colonies. Without Irish statesmanship such ties might not exist. Present-day Ireland outside the Commonwealth provides a liberal, English type of education for many Africans and Asians who, by the irony of history and nationalism, refrain from pursuing British training on British soil but eagerly absorb it on an Irish one. With its many foreign students, Trinity College, established almost 400 years ago by the first Queen Elizabeth to make Irishmen good subjects of England, may be a last, deciding factor in preserving British influence abroad.

How these things have come about are well and stimulatingly told in Mr. McCarthy's account of Irish character and history and civilization. The beauty and charm of Ireland and its people are always evident in pictures of them, as they are in this book. If the struggle to national fulfilment has often seemed tortuous, harrowing and dark, like Ireland's weather, the irrepressible Irish personality everywhere shines through. We are fortunate to have so much of it in the United States. To learn more of Ireland, and of its modern development as well as its heritage and history, should always be an attractive enterprise for Americans. To that end it is a pleasure to introduce this book.

WILLIAM H. TAFT III
former U.S. Ambassador to the Republic of Ireland

To the strains of a local fiddler, a girl in the regional costume joins her partner in a traditional dance for a crowd in front of the Sligo

8

town hall during the annual Fleadh Cheoil, or music festival.

1

In
Island
Isolation

A STRANGER who looked at Ireland on a map of Europe might be surprised to find that it was such a small and isolated country. It seems unlikely that a people like the Irish, known everywhere for their songs and wit, their natural literary, political and military skills, and their unmistakable personality which sets them apart from all other nationalities, should have come from a remote little island cut off in the mists of the North Atlantic from the centres of Old World civilization.

Ireland s isolation at the cloudy crossroads where the warm air of the Gulf Stream clashes against the winds of the Arctic largely explains, however, why the Irish *are* different from other people. Theirs was one of the few nations in Western Europe never invaded by the Romans. The waters around them also kept out, in later centuries, other Continental refinements and helped their 700-year fight against assimilation by the English, which might have failed had Ireland been a part of the British mainland,

9

as are Wales and Scotland. Today these two member countries of the United Kingdom, both of which share a similar Celtic background, feel little identification with Ireland.

"Some of them we may resemble in ways," an Irishman said recently of the Welsh and Scots with a certain aloof pride, "but with none of them could we be easily confused."

But island isolation cannot fully account for whatever it is that makes the Irish so distinct from everybody else; the people of Iceland, for example, are not marked with the contradictions of character that inspired G. K. Chesterton to describe the Irish as romantics whose wars are merry and whose songs are sad—and then to point out elsewhere that they excel as lawyers and soldiers because of their hard-headed realism. Another effect of a country's geography that deeply influences its temperament and spirit is the climate. If the Irish are drawn in tense suspension between bright dreams and dark reality, so is the Irish weather, which is like the weather of no other place on earth.

The weather in Ireland is too often summed up and dismissed as simply wet and cold. The writer George Moore liked to quote a Mayo farmer's complaint that his cottage was damp enough to give rheumatism to a wild duck. But the Irish seldom carry umbrellas as the English do, and the doors and windows of their country houses are always opened wide. Although it rains in Ireland almost every day, the rain seems to spend more time threatening to fall than actually falling, and when it does come, the downpour seldom lasts for more than half

---

THE COMPLEX GAELIC LANGUAGE

The language known as Gaelic, which the people of Ireland themselves refer to as "Irish", is an ancient tongue, one of the Indo-European group to which English also belongs. It is not, however, an easy language for English-speaking persons to master. Its grammar is complex. Gaelic nouns, for example, are like Latin ones in that they change their endings according to their use in the sentence. Because the language has dropped many syllables since it was given a written alphabet in the eighth century, and because multiple-letter combinations can make a single sound, many modern words contain letters which are not pronounced. This volume makes no attempt to utilize accent marks used in the Gaelic alphabet. Below are some common Gaelic words, and some words used in this book, with their phonetic equivalents:

Eire (Ireland): "Airuh"
Erjnn go bragh (Ireland forever): "Airin go braw"
Dail Eireann (Parliament of Ireland): "Dawyl Airun"
Sinn Fein (Ourselves Alone): "Shin Fane"
Aghaidh (face): "Eye"
Fleadh cheiol (music festival): "Flah kyoil"

---

an hour. Then long, glittering beams of sunlight slant through the masses of broken grey and black clouds, and the sky may clear to a bright blue—if it does not immediately close in again, dark and mean and menacing.

Because the sky is always changing, sullen one minute and sparkling with a joyous, dancing brightness a few minutes later, the colours of Ireland's rolling countryside, usually a patchwork of many delicate shades of light and dark green, turn magically into blue, purple or gold or slide into a solemn, almost black, grey. The air, light and stimulating in the morning, may become heavy and depressing in the afternoon and clear again in the evening. In the summer months, when Ireland enjoys late daylight, the setting sun invariably leaves the evening sky streaked with red, pink and yellow, no matter how gloomy the day may have been.

These constant changes in light and atmosphere can lift the Irishman's spirit to a carefree merriment, and then irritate him into touchy impatience with everything and everybody around him, or plunge him into dreamy, lethargic despair. "Your wits cant thicken in that soft moist air . . ." George Bernard Shaw wrote, trying to describe to an Englishman the effects of the Irish climate. "Youve no such colours in the sky, no such lure in the distances, no such sadness in the evenings. Oh, the dreaming! the dreaming! the torturing, heart-scalding, never satisfying dreaming! . . ."

Because the weather weighs so heavily on the consciousness of the Irish, they talk of it endlessly with a quiet defensiveness, as if they were afraid that complaining might make it worse. On a wet day they praise the "softness" of the rain and explain to visitors that the moist coolness makes the admired complexion of young Irish women smooth and fresh. On a partly clear morning, strangers on the street cry happily to each other, "Isn't it a grand day, thanks be to God!" A slight national disapproval of rain shows itself only during the summer hay-making season, when sunlight becomes important to farmers. In the hurling-mad farming county of Tipperary, families end their summer prayers asking God to "beat Cork and save the hay".

The warmth of the Gulf Stream, which keeps Ireland wet, also protects it against extreme cold as its northern latitude discourages extreme summer heat. Except for a few unusual winter freezes in recent years, which some older Irish people attribute not to nuclear tests but to a deflection of the Gulf Stream by the Panama Canal, Ireland's temperatures generally stay between 40° and 60° F. all the year round. On some parts of the south-west coast, in Kerry and on the incredibly exotic Garnish Island in Bantry Bay, there are flourishing growths of tropical plants and palm trees. But on the same shore-line, not many miles to the north of this Gaelic Riviera, on a July day at Lahinch in Clare, an American tourist will stare at the Irish girls sprawled on the beach in brief bikinis and shudder. The air to him feels as cold as Maine in early October.

THE changing colours in the Irish sky light up and darken a variety of sharply contrasting scenic splendours below. Ireland is only about 170 miles wide and 300 miles long, a day's drive from Cork to Malin Head at the northern tip of Donegal, but it crowds into that relatively small area almost every kind of landscape and terrain except a desert.

Almost all the island's shore-line is fringed with steep mountain ranges. In the middle of this saucer, flowing from north to south and dividing it almost evenly in half before turning to the Atlantic at Limerick, is Ireland's great river, the River Shannon. East of the Shannon, spreading from Dublin and the wildly beautiful Wicklow Mountains up into Meath and Westmeath and down into Tipperary and Kilkenny, are rich green, rolling meadow-lands which produce Ireland's superb thoroughbred horses and the hefty cattle that supply Britain with much of its beef. The fertility of this midland region is typified by the Curragh, the centre of Irish horse-racing in Kildare, an astonishing great plain of luxurious thick grass extending over 5,000 acres without a fence or a tree.

THE greenness of the midlands ends as they approach the Shannon and many parts of the countryside along the river's bed turn into flat and lonely brown bogs, with carefully stacked mounds of peat here and there drying for a farm cottage's fireplace. The distant horizons of the bogs are now marked with the cone-shaped smoke-stacks of the Irish Republic's new peat-burning electricity-generating plants.

Western Ireland, on the other side of the Shannon, is a different country altogether, no more like the plentiful midlands than Wyoming is like Wisconsin. This is the rocky and mountainous province of Connaught—Galway, Mayo, Roscommon, Sligo and Leitrim are its counties—where dispossessed Irish Catholics were sent into exile after Oliver Cromwell turned their lands in Meath and Kildare over to English Protestants in the 17th century. "Hell or Connaught" was the choice offered to them. But although the west is poor farming country—the fields under the purple mountain ranges are stony or swampy, bare, treeless and windswept—its Galway and Mayo sea-coast, especially along the peninsula of Connemara, has some of the most spectacular scenic beauty in all of Europe, heightened by the region's atmosphere of unspoiled primitive simplicity and peacefulness that seems to detach it from the rest of the world.

Ireland in the west, the setting for some of John M. Synge's plays and William Butler Yeats's poems, looks more like the misty green, shamrock-bordered out-dated picture-postcard cliché of the Old Sod than do other parts of the country. Thatched cottage roofs, donkey carts and old women wrapped in long black shawls are fading from the midland and southern counties on the other side of the Shannon, but these reminders of bygone days are still seen along the narrow, stone-walled roads in Connaught and in the adjoining northern county of Donegal.

MOST housewives in Mayo and in the shadow of Connemara's dozen peaks, the Twelve Bens, still bake their bread in iron pots, with red coals of smouldering turf on top of the closed lid, and boil their bacon and cabbage in their cottages' fireplaces rather than on stoves. A fisherman putting out to sea from the nine-mile-long fjord of Killary Harbour, the enormous walls of mountains more than 2,000 feet high rising out of the deep water beside him, rows an ancient type of tarred canvas boat called a currach. As his grandfathers did before him, he wears a sweater of white undyed wool, knitted in a distinctive design signifying his family name so that his body can be identified if he is drowned.

About 2,000 people, ignoring the jets from New York, London and Paris that zoom over their heads, persist in living as their ancestors did on the bleak rocks of the Aran Islands in the Atlantic off Galway Bay. They weave wool for their clothing, cure hides for their moccasin-like shoes and grow potatoes in crevices of the islands' solid limestone on thin patches of soil, carried in buckets from the mainland over past centuries or carefully nurtured by mixing beach sand and seaweed.

The old, poetic Gaelic language, dying elsewhere, is making its last stand in western Ireland. A statue of the famous roaming Gaelic storyteller, Padraic O Conaire, sitting on a pile of rocks like a little leprechaun, has been erected on the green in Galway's central square. Most of the offshore islanders do not speak English. Some years ago a group of them came to Belmullet, a small decayed seaport in Mayo, to watch the late Anew McMaster, the famous Irish actor, perform as Hamlet. They were asked later if they were able to understand what McMaster was saying.

"Sure, we didn't understand it at all, but it was lovely to listen to," one of the island women said in Gaelic. "The words dripped off his tongue like cream."

A traveller driving south from Galway into Clare and Limerick on his way to Kerry begins to see an Ireland much different from the one he left behind. As always, he passes on the road farmers driving cattle and sheep to a village fair and wandering bands of tinkers, with their innumerable handsome red-headed children in horse-drawn caravans. But at Ennis he finds new German-owned factories making carpets and sportswear, and a few miles farther on he comes to the vast new industrial complex beside the jet airport at Shannon, where British, German, American, Dutch, South African and Japanese companies, attracted by low labour costs and factory rents and liberal tax concessions, are producing electronic equipment, machine parts, textiles, drilling materials, pianos, synthetic diamonds and transistor radios. A Shannon prospectus says to foreign investors: "In Ireland there is less danger of political upheaval than in any country in the world. Nowhere is the threat of extreme socialism or communism more remote." But an upheaval of another sort occurred recently at Shannon when the prize for excellence in the local national school's compulsory Gaelic language course was won by a little girl who is Japanese.

A YET more startling innovation awaits our traveller in Kerry. In the heart of that celebrated scenic wonderland, Killarney, a West German industrialist named Hans Liebherr has built a factory that makes cranes and excavating machinery. The same concern has also erected in the wild and rustic countryside near the Gap of Dunloe a shockingly modernistic hotel that bothers Irish people more than the crane factory.

The Kerrymen themselves, more practical than most of their countrymen, are inclined

A TRICOLOUR of green, white and orange is the Republic's flag.

A GOLD HARP decorates the ancient green flag of Ireland.

THE UNION JACK is the official emblem of the United Kingdom.

A RED CROSS on a white field is the regional flag of Ulster.

THE FOUR BANNERS OF TWO ISLAND NEIGHBOURS

The unions and divisions of Ireland are reflected in the four flags shown above. The tricolour on the left, first flown in 19th-century rebellions against Britain, is intended to symbolize the unity of the island's people: green for the South, orange for the North. The green flag is older; the harp was an Irish instrument in very early times. The Union Jack, emblem of the United Kingdom of Great Britain, Scotland, Wales and Northern Ireland, carries both the diagonal red cross of Saint Patrick and the red cross of Saint George of England, which is also seen on the Northern Ireland flag (far right). The hand recalls legends about the early conquest of Ireland; the crown symbolizes the British monarchy.

to take a tolerant view of this development. "Scenery is grand," one of them says, "but our young people can't live on it."

West German industry, bringing hope of stemming the tide of young Irish emigration, is more welcomed than the recent influx of West German farmers and retired businessmen who have been buying homes in western and southern Ireland. The Germans frankly admit that they are attracted by the Irish Government's steadfast neutrality and by the prevailing west wind, which they think less likely to carry nuclear fall-out from Europe in the event of war. But they fence off the beaches of their newly acquired waterfront property, and this enrages the hospitable Irish. A wry joke, popular in Dublin, concerns a German settler in Kerry who has become so thoroughly Irish that his sons have gone off to work in England.

The famous scenery of Kerry, particularly in the lake district of Killarney, is different again from the rough and unruly rockiness of Connemara. Killarney is elegant and stately, with the blue waters of its three lakes in a setting of rolling green lawns, forests of tall, graceful trees and massive growths of rhododendrons and other flowering shrubbery. It looks like a carefully landscaped great private estate, which, in fact, it is. Most of the lakeland is made up of the Muckross and Kenmare baronial domains, tended and trimmed over past centuries by battalions of gardeners and foresters.

But even the sea-coast hills of Kerry, along Dingle Bay between Killorglin and Cahirciveen,

where there are no trees at all, have a delicate refinement. Killorglin is the scene of the annual August Puck Fair, three days of merry-making and cattle- and horse-trading when the pubs stay open nearly all night and a beribboned male goat presides as king of the festival on a platform in the market square. One explanation of the honouring of this goat is that, like many Irish ceremonies, it dates back hundreds of years to a battle against English invaders. A stampeding herd of goats gave warning of the enemy's approach and Killorglin has been expressing its gratitude ever since.

DOWN at the southern tip of the Kerry peninsula, overlooking the entrance to the River Kenmare, where smugglers' boats late in the 18th century picked up Irish youths travelling secretly to Catholic seminaries in France and Spain, stands Darrynane, the home of Daniel O'Connell, the emancipator who "found the Irish peasants slaves and left them men". O'Connell's house is empty and falling into ruins, without a marker or signpost on it, a reminder that the young Irish Republic, for all its recent forward strides, has not yet been able to restore all its patriotic shrines. Kilmainham jail in Dublin, where the executed leaders of the 1916 Easter Week rebellion were imprisoned, was also decaying from neglect until a group of private citizens undertook to restore it with their own hands.

As he leaves the Kerry peninsula and resumes his exploration of the rest of Ireland—swinging from Cork across to the Irish Sea at Dublin and up that eastern shore into Ulster—the traveller becomes more aware that he is passing through a very old country, a place that was encrusted, long before Columbus discovered America, with the stony remains of many ages of civilization. To a visitor from Ohio, for example, whose oldest settlement, Marietta, goes back only to 1788, the dates of even the more recent Irish monasteries, castles and towns would seem incredible. The writers of the authoritative *Shell Guide to Ireland* mention casually, for example, that although "there were several churches and monasteries in the area in an early historic period, the story of Dublin as a city does not commence until A.D. 841".

TO an Irishman, this is not really old. At Newgrange in Meath, near Slane Hill where Saint Patrick lit his Paschal fire in 433, there is a Bronze Age burial chamber 4,000 years old. The whole country from Kerry to County Down in Ulster is scattered with prehistoric ring-forts, standing stones and dolmens —large, flat rocks balanced on top of upright supporting boulders or slabs. They are thought to be either the altars of ancient sun worshippers or the inner walls of tombs once covered with earth. The capstone of one dolmen called the Giant's Grave at Kiltiernan, near Dublin, is 23 feet long, 17 feet wide and 6 feet thick. A farmer in the area doubts the theory that this enormous rock was lifted into place above its supporting stones by a hundred or more strong men straining in unison. "When could you get a hundred Irishmen to pull together?" he asks.

Relics of the early Christian era are all over Ireland: ancient Celtic crosses and the ruins of monastic settlements, like Clonmacnois on the Shannon in County Offaly where Saint Ciaran established a school for monks in 548, and where Rory O'Conor, the last High King of Ireland, was buried in 1198 after the Norman invasion. A small sixth-century church, or oratory, looking like an overturned boat with its walls of corbelled stones arching to form a

pointed roof 14 feet high, stands remarkably intact on the Dingle peninsula. The countryside is dotted with the soaring round-towers, some rising to 100 feet, where monks in the ninth and tenth centuries climbed to escape the attacking Danes, pulling up the ladders behind them. Most of the towers are in a much better state of preservation than the surrounding churches and castles that were built hundreds of years later. Their limestone blocks are held firmly in place by a miraculous cement of the Middle Ages whose long-lost formula, the Irish say, contained cockleshells, egg whites, animal manure, ox blood and ox hair, lime, river-bed silt and sand.

But the most stirring ancient sight in all of Ireland is the mighty Rock of Cashel, stronghold of the Kings of Munster, rising high and abruptly over the surrounding green plains of Tipperary. Crowning the heights of the steep rock, where Saint Patrick baptized a King of Munster in 450, are the great grey walls of a 13th-century cathedral and its adjoining archbishop's castle, a 10th-century round-tower and Cormac MacCarthy's gem-perfect little Romanesque chapel, built in 1134, which ranks beside the beautifully illuminated eighth-century *Book of Kells* as one of Ireland's proudest inheritances from its golden Middle Ages.

AERIAL photographs of the rock show that the walls of the cathedral and the older chapel, crowding closely on each other, are built on slightly diverging lines. The chapel was dedicated to Mary. It was oriented on a point of the compass a few degrees north of east so that the rising sun in May, the month of Mary, would shine directly into its altar window, while the cathedral, dedicated to Saint Patrick, was built to face the sun on the morning of the 17th of March.

Ireland's history is divided sharply by the Anglo-Norman invasion of 1170, which separates the earlier golden centuries when the nation, under its own High Kings, was a flourishing centre of ecclesiastical learning, from the later 700-odd years of subjugation under the English. Cashel represents the old Celtic Ireland. It was established as a royal fortress in 730, and after the country was converted, the rock was ruled by leaders who were bishops as well as kings. They produced such works as the *Book of Rights*, a code of laws composed in Gaelic verse. Irishmen like to point out the contrast between the exquisite artistry of Cormac's pre-Norman chapel and the heavy greyness of the Anglo-Norman cathedral built beside it in the rock's later, declining years.

THE early Celtic Irish did not congregate in towns; they were farmers and herdsmen whose only developed settlements were monastic communities, like Clonmacnois, or forts, like Cashel. The handsome castles of Irish feudal estates and the lovely cathedral towns came with the Normans, who also developed the small Scandinavian sea-port bases at Dublin, Cork and Limerick into medieval cities. The traveller today finds those three Irish cities, together with Belfast, each as different from the others as are the east, south, west and north parts of the country where they are respectively located.

Belfast is the least Irish; when the other four fifths of Ireland broke away from the United Kingdom in 1921, Belfast became the capital of the six northern Ulster counties that remained loyal to London because they had little in common with the rebels. It is the only Irish city that is Protestant rather than Roman Catholic (many of Belfast's playgrounds, and all its pubs, are closed on Sunday) and the only one affected by the Industrial Revolution of the 19th century, which boosted its ship-building and textile manufacturing and raised its heavily Scottish population from 25,000 to 350,000 in that period. With its long rows of grimy labourers' houses, Belfast has the very un-Irish look of a hard-worked factory town.

There is little sternness, however, in the look of the pretty Ulster coastal country. The tourist who ventures into this north-east corner of Ireland, seldom mentioned by the travel articles that praise Kerry and Galway, finds himself in

a holiday land of green mountains and long sandy beaches, crowded during the summer months with visitors from England and Scotland who sail, play golf, cycle and bowl on outdoor greens. This is the country where Finn MacCool, the legendary Irish hero, scooped up a vast piece of sod, thereby creating the lake of Lough Neagh, and hurled the sod into the Irish Sea to form the Isle of Man. The Antrim coast road, running along the edge of the water beside the hills and brightly coloured glens of the Antrim Mountains north of Belfast, has views as stunning as those along the Adriatic coast of Italy.

The industrialized North of Ireland, with its new plants which are envied in Dublin, stands as aloof as ever from the Republic. The gulf may be narrowing, but religious differences are still strongly felt. On July 12, Orangeman's Day, the city streets and country roads of Ulster are draped with colourful banners proclaiming allegiance to the Queen, and back-street fences are chalked with anti-papist slogans.

AN American tourist picked up two teenaged hitch-hikers recently near a small temporary bridge on the Ulster border. "What happened to the bridge?" he asked.

"Blown up by them men that blow up the bridges."

"And what men are they?"

The boy eyed the stranger carefully and said, "Don't they call them the I.R.A.?"

The underground Irish Republican Army, which fought the British to win freedom for Ireland and which has never accepted the separateness of Ulster, was officially disbanded by its old leader, President Eamon de Valera. But it is yet alive, although dwindling in numbers, and still has its own strong ideas about how to bring back the partitioned six counties. The same American listened later to a southern Irishman describing an I.R.A. attack on the Ulster town of Omagh a few years ago. "Cork was empty that night," he said.

Cork is the Irish Naples, the throbbing and lively city of the south. It was the hotbed of the revolution. Its main business district, City Hall and the public library were burned in 1920 by British constabulary troops. When a peace-seeking priest in Cork talked against the rebellion, the men and women rose and quietly walked out of the church—returning after the sermon, of course, for the consecration and communion. Resentment against the partition, somewhat softened elsewhere by pleas for tolerance from de Valera, remains strong in Cork and in the smaller provincial western city of Limerick. A crowd of some 30,000 people gathered in Limerick a while ago for the funeral of an I.R.A. youth named Sean South who was killed during a foray into Ulster.

THE capital city of Dublin, the only place in the Republic with traffic and parking problems, is less concerned with old political sores than with present economical needs. To picture Dublin, imagine an old city, rather threadbare, whose public buildings and town houses were built by wealthy aristocrats in the elegant Georgian period before the American Revolution. Like all of Ireland, Dublin was tired and battered from the invasions of Cromwell and William of Orange when it was taken over in the 18th century by a new ruling class of Protestant landowners known as the Anglo-Irish ascendancy, who moved into the city to run the Irish Parliament in its magnificent new building on College Green.

These titled grandees, revelling in their sudden rise to national leadership, hired the best architects and building craftsmen of the day to create an Irish capital city suitably splendid for their cultured taste. During their reign they built the superbly designed Customs House on the River Liffey, Trinity College, the Four Courts and all Dublin's palatial private residences, including the Leinster House—said to be a prototype for the later United States White House. Then in 1800, when prosperous Dublin was spreading in all directions, the Act of Union dissolved Ireland's Parliament and moved its legislature, like those of Wales and Scotland, to London. The boom in Dublin

collapsed and the city came to a standstill. It has not changed much since.

Parts of O'Connell Street, the main Dublin thoroughfare, had to be rebuilt after they were demolished by artillery fire in the 1916 rebellion, but the heart of Dublin, with no skyscrapers and no new motor-ways, remains as it was in the 18th century when Jonathan Swift was Dean of Saint Patrick's Cathedral. The old Parliament House, with its rounded front of stately dark columns, houses the Bank of Ireland. The fine houses of the earls and knights stand undisturbed on Saint Stephen's Green and Merrion Square, even if they are occupied now by Government agencies and by business and professional firms. Other Georgian homes are falling into shabby neglect in poor neighbourhoods, but antiquarian societies are now fighting to keep them from being torn down.

"Ireland is the only civilized-looking country left in Europe," one of the Georgian-house defenders says. "We must keep it that way."

But Ireland, with its roadside directional signs stubbornly printed in Gaelic, finds it increasingly hard to cling to the charms of the past. The country's age-old need—more better-paid work to keep young Irishmen from emigrating—continues to be one of Ireland's most pressing problems. A frightening total of about 400,000 Irish people, mostly young, emigrated in the decade 1952-62.

POLITICAL freedom, after long centuries of dreaming of it and fighting for it, came as a let-down to Ireland. Olivia Robertson, a discerning observer of the Irish character, has compared modern Ireland to a man who has been proposing gallantly for years to an unresponsive woman—and then finds himself unexpectedly accepted. He has never really thought much about what marriage would be like. Now he has a wife and family to support and not much money with which to pay the rent.

The problems brought on by independence were difficult ones, and only today is Ireland getting over the shock of discovering that realization is not as rosy as expectation.

As their donkey waits, children of County Mayo load a cart with peat before taking the sunlit road leading towards their home.

A Quiet Setting for Yesterday's Eventful Dramas

Much of Ireland is sparsely settled today. In the countryside the long, peaceful perspectives are only occasionally broken by the figures of children playing or farm people going about their tasks. The quiet is in a way misleading: the loneliness speaks of centuries of pain and violence. Nothing of the past has been forgotten; the very names of the hills and towns conjure up remembrances of battles and famine. Although at a first glance the landscape appears to be solitary and untouched, closer inspection reveals that every valley, crag and field has been marked by human hands. Even the most blissful pasture, buzzing with sounds of summer, is redolent of bitter memories of war, hunger and emigration. The island's past crowds thickly on every slope.

AN ISOLATED COTTAGE in County Donegal in the north-west is crossed by shifting cloud patterns of light and dark. The simple construction, employing whitewashed walls and thatched roof, is typical of Ireland's west. Although the mountains and jagged coastline of Donegal are barren, the valleys are fertile areas for growing flax and raising sheep.

SEQUESTERED FIELDS, separated into neat rectangles by stone walls, provide a Galway farmer with hay and pasturage. The hilliest part of the land (*background*) is too steep to cultivate.

TROUT FISHING absorbs the attention of a father and his sons in Connemara, County Galway's lake district. In the distance rises the series of peaks known as the Twelve Bens.

Collecting supplies, a group of Aran Islanders moves from shore in a currach, a type of vessel made of wood and tarred canvas in use

for more than 1,500 years. It is as primitive as life in the Islands, one of the last places where Gaelic is still an everyday language.

JUTTING into the sea, Dingle peninsula in County Kerry (*opposite*) is the mainland's westernmost area. Because arable land is scarce in the west, fields are planted to the cliff's edge.

GRAZING on upland pastures, powerful cart-horses roam the Sheeffry hills in County Mayo. Since the 1846 potato famine, pastoral farming has superseded crop-growing in importance.

AN EVENING PERSPECTIVE of Londonderry, an old seaport in Northern Ireland, reveals rich grain-fields which roll right to the edge of the suburbs hard by the peaceful River Foyle.

THE GEORGIAN SYMMETRY of St. Stephen's Protestant Church in Dublin and the formal façades of town houses along Upper Mount Street recall the days of the Anglo-Irish aristocracy.

2

An Elusive, Unmistakable Character

IT is often said that Ireland's most outstanding export is people. Just as often it is observed that descendants of Irish immigrants removed from Ireland for as many as three generations, like the late John F. Kennedy, remain labelled as Irish. "I was born in the United States and so was my father before me but my children are still called Irish," Kennedy's father once protested. "What the hell do we have to do to become Americans?"

In a recent study of the question, the essayist V. S. Pritchett decided that the Irish preserve their singularity in lands other than their own because they constitute a great world-wide secret society, dedicated to protecting their racial imagination. It may be more simply that the Irish stand apart from long force of habit; after centuries of resisting assimilation by the British at home, they are now slow to accept it abroad. But whatever the cause, clannishness—like that of the Kennedy family—is the deepest trait of the Irish and many of their other characteristics stem from it.

Togetherness is carried to extremes in Ireland. Despite its good Atlantic harbours, the country lacks a sizeable fishing industry or a substantial commercial maritime fleet largely because Irishmen refuse to stay away from home overnight. In the west of Ireland, *bon voyage* parties for young people going off to work in England or emigrating to America are called "wakes" because they are as sad as burials. Weddings are often heartbreaking ordeals for the families involved. A foreign visitor in Dublin recently noticed a young woman in travelling clothes standing alone in front of a hotel while three men were weeping bitterly with their arms around each other in the hotel doorway.

"It's just a wedding," a passer-by explained. "That's the bride and there's the groom saying good-bye to his father and his grandfather."

SUCH intense devotion to parents is as responsible as economic strain and emigration for modern Ireland's notoriously delayed marriages and its high population of bachelors and spinsters. Before performing a wedding ceremony in Roscommon a few years ago, the village priest had to read up on the ritual because he had long forgotten it. Anyone looking at the wedding pictures in Irish newspapers might be struck by the age of the bridegroom, usually in his 30s, and then notice that the bride, too, is not young. All over Ireland, and in many Irish communities in Britain, America and Australia, long-engaged couples will wait for a mother or father to die before they marry. It is unthinkable for the Irish to put love and romance before family obligations. There is always a son who stays at home to run the farm for his ageing parents, and he hesitates to disturb the authority of his mother by bringing a wife into the house.

The attachment between an Irish mother and her son is strong. The father is the head of the closely knit family, and although he never pushes a perambulator or washes dishes, he takes charge of the boys when they reach the age of seven or eight. In many Irish country homes, as in Japan, or even in the farm belt of the American Mid-West, the housewife does not eat dinner until the men have left the table. She has no part in her husband's social life; he goes off with his sons and other men to the village pub and to football and hurling matches while she stays home with her daughters. In churches in small towns, the men and boys sit apart from women and girls at Sunday Mass.

But within the family circle, the mother has the prestige and influence of a queen, and she intercedes powerfully for her son in disputes between him and his father. She sees to it that her son gets the best cut of the meat, sometimes better than the one she serves to her husband. She secretly slips him money for a dance. She hates the thought of his leaving home to marry, and in many cases, so does he.

The bonds of an Irish family are deep between brothers and sisters and their uncles, aunts and grandparents. A courageous bride who does venture into a home with parents-in-law is likely to find herself also caring for her husband's widowed aunt and elderly grandfather and perhaps his 50-year-old bachelor brother. It is a disgrace for a family to let old relatives live alone and a scandalous shame to put a grand-uncle or an aged aunt among strangers in a nursing home or public institution.

THE loyalty of an Irishman to his brother is illustrated by a conversation between two farmers in a pub at Dunaff in Donegal. One of the men said that he knew somebody who could leap 15 feet backwards. "That's a physical impossibility," the other man said. "There isn't a human being on this earth capable of performing such a feat. I'm surprised that you should stand there and expect me to swallow such a desperate falsehood. Now tell me, will you not, who did you ever see jump backwards 15 feet?"

"Your own brother Dinny."

"My brother Dinny? Aye, sure, of course, Dinny could do it. Many's the time I've seen Dinny give a jump backwards not only 15 feet but sometimes 20 and 23 feet."

A priest in Kilkenny, now in his 70s, has been harbouring a resentment against an older brother in New York for more than 50 years because of what he considers an inexcusable breach of family loyalty: "When he left home to go to America, he promised me on his knees that he would come back for my ordination as a priest three years later. He never came. Don't tell me it might have been hard for him to make the trip. Our poor old Aunt Mary made it, travelling alone all the way from St. Paul, Minnesota."

AS warmly cheerful and charming as they are, the Irish self-consciously hide their deep emotions beneath a careful composure for sake of appearances. "There's no kissing in public in this country and none at home either if the children are present," an Irishwoman says. But their upright propriety melts into helpless anguish when death takes away a member of the family. At a funeral in Cork a middle-aged man cried out as the coffin was carried from the church, "Oh, Gran-da! Gran-da! You're dead and gone! Who'll jam me bread now?" At wakes in Galway and Sligo, women relatives and neighbours take turns during the night "keening", wailing Gaelic ejaculations of grief for the dead like those in the dialogue of Synge's *Riders to the Sea*. ("He's gone now, God spare us, and we'll not see him again. He's gone now, and when the black night is falling I'll have no son left in the world.")

However, the old traditional Irish wake, with several nights of drinking, reminiscing and storytelling, is now only a remembrance of the past in Ireland. The Church has discouraged it in recent years because it became too social, too much of an expensive hardship for many bereaved families and the butt of too many jokes.

The present procedure is to wake the body for only one night at home. Then it is taken to the church, where there is a brief service with a rosary on the second evening, with the funeral on the following morning. The Irish funeral is an important event in the community, attended by people from surrounding counties and reported at length in the local newspaper with paragraphs of lavish praise for the dead person. ("Deeply devoted to his family, he took a passionate interest in their happiness and well-being.") Sometimes, in keeping with the customs of older generations, a group of friends will come forward after the Requiem Mass to dismiss the hearse and carry the coffin from the church to the cemetery on their shoulders.

Their staunch respect for parental authority, together with their acceptance of the moral doctrines of the Roman Catholic Church, has made the Irish law-abiding, conventional and conservative. There is little crime in Ireland. Women feel at ease alone on the Dublin streets late at night, and it is common to see respectable matrons hitch-hiking on country roads. An elderly lady who lives alone on the main street of a midland town leaves the key inserted on the outside of her front door's spring-lock day and night so that callers can enter without summoning her from the kitchen. Dublin and Belfast have their quota of gum-chewing and twisting teenaged girls with teased hair and tight skirts, and boys with sideburns and narrow, sharply pointed shoes, but Ireland has no juvenile delinquency worth mentioning—and no night-life after its bars close at 11.30.

The inborn esteem of the Irish for moral law and authority enables them to submit to government restrictions that would outrage liberals in other Western democracies. The constitution of the Republic, drawn up by Eamon de Valera in 1936, forbids divorce and provides for a censorship that has banned even the books of Graham Greene and other Catholic novelists, and forced them to be sold under the counter in Dublin. It is illegal for an Irish chemist to sell any kind of contraceptive. The more lurid large-circulation British Sunday newspapers are required to remove racy sex stories from editions sent to Ireland.

A CHAMPION of individual rights and freedom who tried to change these constitutional laws, moreover, would find most of the Irish against him. "But you must remember that this Constitution was drawn to suit the Irish people, who are very strict in matters of morals," writes Robert Briscoe, the Jewish ex-Lord Mayor of Dublin, in his memoirs,

For the Life of Me. "It is generally considered that the Puritans of America were the most uncompromising moralists of all time and that Roman Catholics are distinctly flexible in this respect. I assure you this only applies to Catholics in Latin countries. The Irish Catholic is as puritanical as any passenger on the *Mayflower* and de Valera in notably straight-laced, even among Irish Catholics. Indeed for purity of mind and rectitude of conduct he would make Elder Brewster seem a libertine by contrast. There are many in Ireland, the majority by far, who are of Dev's mind about these matters of morality and that is why the censorship provisions in our Constitution are right for them."

DISCUSSING the moral code of the Irish recently, Briscoe recalled the civil war in 1922 when, as one of de Valera's Republicans, his name was placed on a list of enemies whom Free State soldiers were to shoot on sight. Walking unarmed one day in Dublin, he came upon a Free State officer, Sean MacEoin, who recognized him and drew a gun. Briscoe turned his back on MacEoin and walked safely away.

"I was sure that no Irishman like MacEoin would shoot anybody in the back and I was right," Briscoe said. "When I see Sean nowadays, I thank him and he loudly curses the high principles that kept him from pulling the trigger."

Ireland's stern moral standards, more repressive in the small country towns than in the cities, have prompted many restless young people to move to England; they are as anxious for excitement as for better-paying jobs. "As teenagers, my sisters and I would walk a mile from our house to the main road, just to sit on a wall and watch the motor-cars drive by," says a young woman who grew up on a farm in County Limerick. "And some evenings there weren't many motor-cars."

Puritanical though they may be, the Irish take a quite tolerant view of what other nations have long regarded as the island's most conspicuous moral problem, the Irishman's proverbial "weakness for the drink". The Irish-born playwright George Bernard Shaw, among others, has suggested that the Irishman finds his imagination too tortuous to bear without whiskey. The Irish deny this allegation. They point out that habitual drinkers in Ireland vastly prefer the country's black Guinness stout and lager beer to whiskey, and that these brews are not the drink of a tormented alcoholic. They blame modern Irish literature and literary biography, so filled with figures like James Joyce's father, lifting a convivial glass with friends in a pub while his family is being evicted, for making the singing alcoholic almost as much a symbol of Ireland in non-Irish minds as the shamrock and the shillelagh.

The average Irishman sees nothing especially deplorable in the fact that a village like Milltown Malbay in County Clare, with a population of 650 people, has 27 licensed pubs, or public bars. The pub plays an important role in Irish social life. Unlike the English or Americans, the Irishman seldom drinks at home, except on special festive occasions—partly because his wife, like most middle-class Irishwomen, is likely to be a teetotaller. He prefers having his glass of stout in the male company that he finds in a pub, and so he spends an hour or two there in the evening.

SMALL villages with only one or two butchers' shops or tobacconists and sweet shops will have several pubs because there are different types to suit different male tastes. Some are noisy, filled with songs and jovial chatter, and others are quiet and dignified. The pub-going habit in Ireland is not confined to the working class as it has tended to be in Britain. Many wealthy socialites, who live in large, servant-staffed country homes—and whose wives join them in a drink—spend an hour before dinner with their friends in a village pub.

"It's much more entertaining than sitting by ourselves in the living-room at home," the wife of a millionaire horse-breeder in County Meath says. "In the pub, we hear all the local news and gossip. Then we go to our homes for dinner. Sometimes we return to the pub later for a nightcap. We Irish feel that drinking alone at home is dull and antisocial."

The Irish distaste for drinking in the quiet of the home used to make the annual St. Patrick's Day dog-show in Dublin one of the year's most popular sporting events. Until the law was changed a few years ago, pubs were closed on St. Patrick's Day, a holy day in Ireland, but one bar at the dog-show was allowed to stay open during that event. Consequently the show was stormed by crowds of non-dog-lovers from all over Dublin. One year Brendan Behan, fighting the crush around the bar, stepped on the paw of a terrier on its way to the judging circle. The burly dramatist glared at the contestant's owner and said, "Now isn't this a silly place to bring a dog?"

During a discussion of the function of the Irish pub, a Dubliner cited a memorable line spoken by Barry Fitzgerald in *The Quiet Man*, the Academy Award-winning film comedy of Irish country life directed by John Ford. Fitzgerald, on his way to a pub, declares, "I think I'll go and join me comrades and talk a little treason."

"The fellow who wrote that line knew Ireland," the Dubliner said. "He makes his character out to be heading for the pub not so much because he wants a drink but mainly because he wants to talk before an audience. That's the Irish pub, a stage for the orator, and that's an Irishman—a performer who loves to hear himself talk. Treason, of course, is now out as a timely topic of discourse because Ireland, sad to say, has won her political freedom, leaving a great yawning gap in his repertoire, but he finds enough other things to talk about until the bar-tender shuts off the lights and pushes him into the street."

The long conversations in Ireland are not confined to the atmosphere of pubs or to men; they go on everywhere at all hours between people of both sexes and all ages. In the morning, hauling his wagon of milk churns from the creamery, the farmer stops his tractor in

IRELAND'S COUNTIES have special importance. Although their political significance is slight, they receive strong emotional allegiance from their inhabitants, and this is true also in Great Britain's six Northern counties (*dark shading*) which are commonly known as Ulster. The other provinces, hangovers from the ancient kingdoms, are much less vital in Irish life.

the road, turns off the motor, and listens, leaning on the steering-wheel, while a neighbour woman talks to him from her cottage doorway. Two small, red-cheeked boys, with their books in sachels strapped on their backs, talk wildly all the way home from school. A girl of 20, in a coat of the bright royal blue that seems to be the Irishwoman's favourite colour, leans out of a window in the Limerick–Dublin bus while it is stopped in Monasterevin, beckons to a young man standing near by and chatters to him, smiling and laughing. A Frenchman or a Welshman might misunderstand her intentions, but the Irish youth knows that she is talking only to pass the time until the bus starts moving again.

The stage Irishman is said to be a cliché of fiction, but Ireland is full of sly Barry Fitzgeralds and crisp, swaggering James Cagneys, and every neighbourhood has its Brendan Behan, eager to confide a few thousand choice words that just occurred to him. The Irish fondle a word and rub it and polish it before carefully arranging it in a sentence. "In these beautiful mountains, heaven is a foot and a half above the height of a man," a Kerrywoman says. A priest watches an elderly and ailing parishioner hobbling weakly from the church and says, "He's walking slow but he's going fast." An old man in a crowded pub holds up a pint glass of Guinness and says, "If this be a ghost that I see here in my hand before me, I hope it reappears again soon." Pritchett, in his essay on the Irish character, tells of seeing a huge political sign, "Vote for Duffey", on a wall near Dublin and next to it, added by the opposition in letters running for more than a hundred yards, "And Ireland's dead will rise and curse you."

Two strangers carry on a conversation in a hotel dining-room with a white-haired, red-faced Irishman seated alone at a near-by table. When they leave, one says that it was a pleasure to talk to him.

"I would say the same to you, sir," the elderly Irishman replies, "but it would sound repetitive."

THE Gaelic wit shines in sharp retorts and deflating sarcasm. Asked if the cream is fresh, a waitress says, "If it was any fresher, it would be grass." A street-corner loafer eyes the brand new pigskin gloves of a lucky companion who has made a big killing at the races and remarks sneeringly, "Isn't it curious that when a man comes into wealth, suddenly his hands get cold?" An auctioneer named McGrath, trying to sell a black iron cooking-pot, spots the town's Protestant minister in the audience and yells at him, "Now this nice round little pot would make a lovely bell for your church."

"With your tongue in it, Mr. McGrath?" the minister says.

A Canadian who lives in Dublin is dissatisfied with the education his children are receiving in their Irish national elementary school; they are taught, he says, too much by rote and memory drilling. But the talk of Irish labourers and farmers and young errand-boys and shop-girls, with only a few years of such education, displays an erudition and command of language that astonishes foreigners today as it astonished William Makepiece Thackeray in Cork in 1842. ("I listened to two boys almost in rags: they were lolling over the quay balustrade, and talking about *one of the Ptolemys*! and talking very well, too . . . with a great deal of fire and eloquence.") Today a taxi-driver in Cork recites Robert Burns, not in modern schoolbook English, but in Burns's original difficult Scottish-Gaelic dialect. Kathleen Cavanagh, proprietress of a greengrocer's in the grey medieval town of Birr, lectures to a visitor on the Brehon Laws of early Celtic Ireland, pausing now and then to urge a customer to try the new Duke of York potatoes.

THE clannishness of the Irish brought on an intense wave of nationalism when the old Free State won self-government from the British in 1921. Only now, under economic need for foreign friendships and the passing of the older revolutionaries, is that aloofness wearing thin. One less-than-successful effort to bring back the glory of ancient independent Ireland was de Valera's struggle to revive the Gaelic language, the tongue spoken by the Irish Catholic peasants until 150 years ago.

The Constitution drawn up in 1936 declared Gaelic to be the national and "first official" language, and it became a compulsory subject in the schools. An earlier Gaelic-revival movement, which coincided with the beginnings of the Irish drive for independence, had been warmly welcomed by the Irish people because it was a gesture of defiance against the British. But after the British were gone, the realistic Irish saw little to be gained from speaking a language understood by nobody else in the shrinking modern world. Besides, Gaelic is difficult for English-speaking Irish to master. Its alphabet is strange and its words have letters that are not pronounced: Dun Laoghaire, the Gaelic name for the town of Dunleary, is pronounced "Doon Laye-reh". The official Gaelic title for the Irish Prime Minister, *Taoiseach*, is sounded "tea-shook".

WITH characteristic Irish stubbornness, de Valera persisted in promoting the old language while he was leading the Government in the 1930s and 1940s. If two doctors applied for a public-health office, the appointment would go automatically to the one who spoke Gaelic, even if his qualifications were inferior. School-children were given extra credit in history or geography examinations if their papers were written in Gaelic. Gaelic scholars like Frank O'Connor, who was a leading Irish writer, were amused by the Government's attempts to put Gaelic names on things like the Irish Hospital Sweepstakes lottery, which became, in literal Gaelic, The Little Sweeping-Brushes of the Hospitals of Ireland.

Gaelic is still required in the schools but Sean Lemass, who succeeded de Valera as the Prime Minister in 1959, indicated that he was far more concerned about Ireland's economic future than its linguistic heritage; he was not anxious to put a language barrier in the way of foreign investors who were bringing industry into the country. So the Gaelic revival, never really very strong, is dwindling fast. Only in parts of the west coast, where English was never spoken, is Gaelic still used in daily conversation. It is now hard to believe that as late as 1541, when Henry VIII had himself named King of Ireland—because "the Irish have the foolish opinion that the Bishop of Rome is King of Ireland"—the proclamation had to be translated into Gaelic so that the Irish peers in the Dublin Parliament could understand it.

But Ireland's attachment to the past is so strong that even young people, who admit that the speaking of Gaelic is ridiculously impractical, hate to see their old language go. "When you go to Galway and hear people speaking Irish, you feel deeply ashamed of yourself for not understanding what they're saying," one Dublin youth says.

The Republic of Ireland, of course, is the only English-speaking country that is Roman Catholic. And within the world-wide Catholic Church, it stands apart from other Catholic countries because of the special burning zeal that shines in the Irish people's faith. The Irishman can never be as casual and relaxed in his religious belief as a devout French, Italian or English Catholic can be; he is too seriously and anxiously concerned with the hereafter. One of the recent Italian Popes is said to have remarked, "Isn't Irish Catholicism a terrifying thing?"

Worship in Ireland is not postponed until Sunday. Most families kneel together every evening to say the rosary at home, and there are people in the churches at all hours attending novenas, benediction, and special spiritual retreat and mission services, making the stations of the cross or merely paying a quick visit to light a holy candle. The Church is the one thing that comes before obligations to the beloved family. The mother who is reluctant to see her son married will never raise her voice in protest if he decides to go off to Africa as a missionary for the rest of his life. Yet with all this constant devotion, Irish men and women are always possessed with the feeling that they are not doing enough for God.

STRIVING for extra gifts of grace, they are continually making pilgrimages and other special acts of penance and sacrifice. More than half a million Irish wear the Sacred Heart pin of the Pioneers, which means that, purely as a religious offering of self-denial, they have made a vow never to take an alcoholic drink. The Pioneers are not reformed drinkers; most of them took their pledge in childhood, or in their early teens, and have never tasted alcohol.

Anyone who tries to analyse the Irish character finds himself confronted with baffling contradictions. With all their intense religious devotion the Irish are superstitious people, believers in ghosts and fairies and good-luck charms. A mother who hears her son's good looks praised by a visitor hastens to sew a small bag of salt to the child's coat to protect him from being stolen by "the little people".

"I don't believe in them," an Irishman will say about fairies, "but they are there."

Despite their ready supplies of wit and humour, the Irish are quick to take offence when they are laughed at, and for all their pride in their countrymen's accomplishments, they acknowledge a large amount of truth in Samuel Johnson's often-quoted observation: "The Irish are a fair people; they never speak well of one another." ("He's made a brilliant success as a surgeon in Dublin, but I've been told he never sends a penny to his poor old sick uncle over in Ballacolla.") The Irish are famous for their warm hospitality: soup and a steak are put before a visitor at 10.30 at night despite his protests that he has already had dinner. But as one student of the Irish personality has written, in such a small country, where gossip travels fast, hospitality is not only a virtue; it can also be a precaution. The housewife may be afraid that someone will say of her, "She never asked me if I had a mouth on me."

THE Irish are given to sudden and perverse moods of suspicion or flaring anger. Ireland itself, much to its surprise, was declared a republic in 1948 through a fit of temper.

Until that time, under the leadership of de Valera, Ireland had retained association with the British Commonwealth as a self-governing free state. Although he wanted Ireland to become a republic eventually, de Valera felt that a complete break from the Commonwealth would wipe away any remaining hope of recovering the six partitioned Irish counties of the North that had remained part of the United Kingdom in 1921.

In 1948 de Valera's Fianna Fail party lost control of Parliament. The opposition leader, John A. Costello, became Prime Minister in a coalition government. After he took office, Costello went to Canada to take part in a Commonwealth bar-association conference. The conference members were entertained one evening by the Governor-General of Canada, Field-Marshal Earl Alexander of Tunis. Alexander is a northern Irish Protestant, born in County Tyrone, the son of an earl with little sympathy for the Catholic rebels of the south. He did not speak to Costello.

Leaving the dinner in a rage, Costello immediately summoned reporters and announced that he was breaking all ties with the British Commonwealth—and therefore, of course, with Northern Ireland—and that he would make Ireland an independent republic.

THE Prime Minister's abrupt announcement left the Irish in Dublin open-mouthed with astonishment. His own party, the Fine Gael, had been advocating a closer union with the Commonwealth. His opposition, de Valera's Nationalists, who had fought for a republic in the civil war, were in no position to object to Costello's proposal, but privately the status of a republic, erecting a higher barrier between them and the six Northern counties, was the last thing they wanted. But having publicly committed himself, Costello had no choice but to put a bill before the Irish Parliament asking for a republic.

"The Dail ratified Costello's unilateral declaration," wrote Robert Briscoe, a member of the legislature at that time, as he is now. "We had to. He had made us look foolish enough in the eyes of the world without the stupidity of disavowing our Prime Minister. . . . But the timing of it and the manner of it can only be put down to personal pique."

And so it was that the Republic of Ireland, the dream of the Irish for centuries, finally came into being at a time when nobody particularly wanted it—because of an Irishman's unpredictable personality.

Concluding hours of horse-bargaining, the buyer and seller join hands with a go-between at Puck Fair in Killorglin, County Kerry.

An Expressiveness Attuned to Whimsy and Wit

One way to gauge the temperament of a nation is to listen to its talk. The Irish personality is not in the words themselves but in the tone of voice. Hyperboles are delivered with a guileless inflection; wondrous events are related with hushed admiration; foolishness is crushed with the laconic sting of a question. Each individual cultivates his own style of conversation, and each region has its verbal idiosyncrasies. Yet wherever words are exchanged, whether between two cronies in a pub, a priest and a penitent in confession, or a mother and son in their hillside cottage, the language exposes quick imagination and wide-ranging association of thought. The Irish tongue records every nuance of a rich fancy.

33

*PILGRIMS annually ascend
a gaunt peak to commemorate Saint
Patrick's trials and good works*

AT THE SUMMIT of the mountain, Croagh Patrick in County Mayo, thousands of the devout, some of them barefoot, wait to hear sermons in Gaelic and English on the last Sunday of July.

ON THE TRAIL that reputedly traces Saint Patrick's ascent during his 40-day fast in A.D. 441, Catholics climb the 2,510-foot height, stopping to perform the traditional stations.

BEFORE AN ORATORY built in 1905 on the site of a ruined mountain-top shrine, Communion is offered at dawn. The annual pilgrimage draws priests and laymen from all over the world.

35

A WHITEWASHED COTTAGE of three small rooms on one level (*opposite*) is the home of Mrs. Mary Sharkey in County Donegal. Her son Patrick repairs the thatched roof as she knits.

THE SPOTLESS INTERIOR is heated by a peat-burning fire and oven. As Patrick pours himself a cup of tea, Mrs. Sharkey sits by the curtained alcove which serves as her bedroom.

Testimony to ancient struggles, the prehistoric fort of Dún Aonghus guards the Aran Islands. The stone fragments were placed to make

access to the inner walls (background) dangerous for invaders.

3

The Bitter Years

THE Irish did not acquire the habit of writing down their legends until they were encouraged to do so by the first Christian missionaries 400 years after the Crucifixion, but then, as now, they were a story-loving people, well fed for generations on glorious tales of their country's past. Not long after the missionaries' arrival, they produced a literature of folklore describing in vivid detail the Ireland of earlier centuries.

So it is that although factual Irish history does not begin until the Christian era, we have an imaginative, highly coloured picture of Ireland in its pagan infancy, showing ancient kings who were surrounded by law-makers, soldiers, musicians and poets and who presided over legislative and cultural assemblies. They were great days; the legendary kingdoms of Ireland were politically and militarily strong, and the land was soon to become a centre of learning and the arts. It was Ireland's tragedy that the days of glory were not to endure; the triumphal years were to be followed by protracted centuries of degradation, persecution and exploitation.

At the time of Christ, Ireland was divided into provincial kingdoms with the same names that those areas bear today—Ulster, Munster, Leinster and Connaught, with the additional royal state of Meath, later taken into Leinster.

The early rulers were Gaelic Celts, with blond and reddish hair, who came to Ireland about 350 B.C. carrying iron weapons that enabled them to subdue the earlier inhabitants, a people from northern Spain who were armed with bronze. One of the most famous kings was Cormac MacArt of the line of Conn, who fortified and enlarged the ancient castle on the sacred hill of Tara, near what is now Dublin, and was supported by a renowned force of warriors called the Fianna, under the command of the legendary hero, Finn MacCool.

To qualify for membership in the Fianna, a recruit had to memorize 12 books of poetry and run through a thick forest, leaping over branches as high as his forehead and stooping under limbs as low as his knees without snapping a twig or tearing off a leaf. He also had to be able to pull a thorn out of his foot without breaking his stride.

THE next famous king after Cormac MacArt in Irish legend was Niall of the Nine Hostages, who ruled at Tara from A.D. 380 to 405, and whose descendants, the O'Neills, were lords of Ulster until 1603. Niall made a series of attacks on Britain and Normandy, then under declining Roman colonial government, and threatened for a while to conquer Wales and Scotland.

It is said that on one of these Irish raids against Britain, Niall's invaders brought back with them to Ulster a young prisoner named Patrick, a Latin-speaking Roman subject whose family was Christian. After several years as a sheep-herding slave in Ireland, Patrick escaped to the Continent, where he studied for the priesthood. In 432 he came back to Ireland as a bishop, charged with converting that nation to Christianity, a task that he carried out with spectacular success.

The acceptance of Saint Patrick's faith by the turbulent and mystic-minded Gaels changed the whole character of Ireland. The island became in the dark ages Western Europe's centre of ecclesiastical learning, a land of monasteries that attracted students from all over the Continent and sent out missionaries, theological teachers and scholars to France, Germany, Austria and Switzerland, and even as far as Russia. Irish monks were in demand everywhere as Latin scribes whose skilled penmanship could preserve classical works of literature. At home, the monks produced the beautifully illuminated Latin scripts of the world-famous books of Kells and Durrow and wrote Celtic poems, romances, epics and histories in Gaelic, making Ireland the first European land north of Italy to produce a literature in its native language.

YET while Ireland flourished as a centre of monastic culture engrossed in art and literature, it declined in political and military power. After Niall's death, there was no strong ruler or central government; the *Ard Ri*, or High King, at Tara was merely the chairman of a council of independent provincial kings who often defied him. In the ninth and 10th centuries, the island was easily overrun by savage seafaring Danish and Norwegian marauders, whose fleets were terrorizing England and Normandy at the same time.

The Scandinavians came first as pirate raiders, rowing up the Shannon and other rivers in their shallow-draught longboats, plundering monastic settlements while the frightened monks cowered above reach in the high Irish roundtowers. Then the Norsemen began to stay, building and fortifying the first towns in Ireland—Dublin, Cork, Limerick, Wexford and Waterford—and marrying Irish women. Such names as Loughlan and Doyle indicate Scandinavian origin. By the middle of the 10th century the Norsemen held great areas of Ireland.

The Norse dominance was finally broken by King Brian Boru, the Irish counterpart of

Alfred the Great of England. In a series of bold military challenges, Brian drove the Danes out of Munster and captured their Dublin stronghold. Overcoming other Irish contenders to the throne he became in 1002 the first—and the last—undisputed native Christian King of all Ireland. Brian spent the next 10 years constructing fortresses and highways, and rebuilding churches and monasteries destroyed by the Scandinavians.

But Brian had made the mistake of marrying the beautiful but treacherous Gormflath, mother of Sitric, the half-Danish ruler of Dublin. Gormflath talked Brian into letting Sitric retain command of Dublin and plotted with her son and her brother, Maelmora, the provincial King of Leinster, to stage an uprising against Brian. She made a deal with Sigurd the Stout, Danish leader of the Orkney Islands, offering to marry him if he would send troops to Sitric's support. After some thought, Sigurd agreed to the proposition.

Brian was by then an old man of 74, but he marched his army from the royal camp at Kincora on the Shannon and met the combined Dublin–Leinster–Orkney force near Clontarf on the outskirts of Dublin on Good Friday, 1014. The fighting began at sunrise and lasted until sunset, a wild and bloody hand-to-hand struggle in which 20,000 men, the Irish in light linen tunics and the Danes in chain mail, slashed at each other with heavy swords and axes.

DESPITE his age, Brian had wanted to take command on the field, but his eldest son persuaded him to wait out the battle in a near-by tent. In the evening, when the beaten Danes began to flee, leaving 7,000 dead behind them, one of their leaders rushed past Brian's bodyguard and killed the King in his own tent.

The costly victory kept Ireland in the hands of the Irish—but only until the arrival of the Normans 150 years later.

These hardened conquerors, who had added England to their French possessions in 1066, were brought to Ireland by a disgruntled King of Leinster, Dermot MacMurrough, who sought their help in his fight for national power. But the Normans would probably have come anyway, sooner or later. Almost 20 years earlier, the Norman King of England, Henry II, had formally requested—and been granted—the Pope's permission to move into "irreligious" Ireland. Hungry for new baronial estates, Henry and his swashbuckling earls and knights had been eyeing Ireland for some time.

THE main Norman expeditionary force invited by Dermot landed near Waterford in 1170 under the command of the Earl of Pembroke, known as Strongbow. Although they spoke the French of Normandy, Pembroke and his companions had grown up in Wales, where the original Norman invaders of England had been given a free rein.

Most of these Norman Welsh felt little loyalty to the British King. After they had taken Waterford and Dublin, they urged Pembroke to break away from Britain and establish an independent Norman monarchy in Ireland.

But Pembroke was too hesitant and too wary of the hot-tempered Henry Plantagenet to try such a move. The King himself came to Ireland in the following year with an army of 4,000 men and 500 knights to stake his claim on the island and make it a part of his kingdom. Ignoring Rory O'Conor, reigning as Ireland's High King, Henry divided the land between the Normans and a few native provincial kings who agreed to pay annual tributes to Britain.

Henry also won over the Irish Catholic hierarchy; a synod at Cashel in 1171 abolished Gaelic liturgies and decreed that divine offices "shall be celebrated according to the usage of the Church of England".

Thus the pattern was set. British rule was to be enforced on Ireland for the next seven centuries. As in England and Wales, however, the Norman conquerors had to fight for the lands assigned to them by the Crown. Their grim castle fortresses sprang up all over the countryside. Outside their walls local wars flared between the mounted soldiers of the earls in suits of mail and conical iron helmets, and the clansmen of native chiefs. But eventually the Normans became, as the saying goes, more Irish than the Irish themselves; the Burkes, Joyces, Fitzgeralds, Roches and Barrys were all originally Norman families. But that merger was a long time in the making. For centuries, there was little but hatred between British and Irish.

When the first Parliament of Ireland was formed late in the 13th century, only English colonists were allowed in it. Native Irish were excluded and parliamentary discussions were carried on in English and Norman French instead of Gaelic, the national language of Ireland at that time.

THE British stirred up more resentment in 1366 by enacting the Statutes of Kilkenny, which were intended to keep Anglo-Normans in Ireland from adopting "the manners, fashion and language of the Irish enemies". These laws, in effect for more than two centuries, made it illegal for the English to inter-marry with the Irish, and even to admit Irish musicians and storytellers to their households. Any English subject heard speaking the Irish language was liable to have his land confiscated.

The hatred between the British and the Irish erupted into a fanatical holy war after the Protestant Reformation when Henry VIII and his Protestant successors tried to impose the practices of the new Church of England on Roman Catholic Ireland.

One of the first of Ireland's bloody religious uprisings broke out against Henry's daughter, Elizabeth I, in Munster in 1579. The Irish leader, Sir James Fitzmaurice, was killed, and a force of some 700 Spanish and Italian soldiers, sent by the Catholic Philip II of Spain and Pope Gregory XIII, was ruthlessly massacred near Dingle by the Queen's colonial troops, headed by Lord Grey and Sir Walter Raleigh. In reprisal for the rebellion, Elizabeth confiscated 200,000 acres of Catholic-owned land in south-west Ireland and turned the land over to Englishmen—a practice that was to become standard in the next two centuries. One tract was given to Raleigh, and it was here that he

planted the first Irish potato, destined to bring the country as much suffering and tragedy as it endured throughout the centuries of religious persecution.

Then came the last stand of Gaelic Catholic aristocracy against Elizabethan oppression. A nine-year war under two able Irish leaders, Hugh O'Neill, Earl of Tyrone, and Red Hugh O'Donnell, ended in famine and defeat. It was followed in 1607 by the sad "Flight of the Earls" into foreign exile. The departure of O'Neill, the last titled descendant of Niall, with some 98 other Northern Irish Catholic leaders, opened the way for Britain to establish the Ulster Plantation—a settlement of Scottish Presbyterians and English Protestants in colonies in the counties of the North. This north-east corner of Ireland, still loyal to the Crown today, was the only part of the country where the British were successful in introducing Protestantism—and Irish Catholic historians are quick to point out that it was done by colonization rather than by conversion. "They had to import them," one Irishman says.

ANOTHER savage, exhausting Protestant-Catholic war erupted in 1641 and continued for more than a decade. In August 1649, Oliver Cromwell, the stern Puritan leader of the temporarily kingless British Government, landed at Dublin with an expertly trained army of 20,000 men. He was determined to extinguish the spirit of rebellion for ever. Cromwell and his soldiers displayed a zealous cruelty. They killed almost the entire population of the east-coast town of Drogheda—civilian men, women and children as well as the defending soldiery. "It has pleased God," Cromwell wrote, "to bless our endeavours at Drogheda . . . the enemy were about 3,000 strong in the town . . . I believe we put to the sword the whole number of the defendants. I wish that all honest hearts may give the glory of this to God alone, to whom indeed the praise of this mercy belongs."

Cromwell's punitive expedition terrified Ireland for almost three years. Some 30,000 Irish soldiers in the armies that surrendered to him

EARLY IRELAND

Churches founded by St. Patrick — Monasteries flourishing in the 6th century

Important events and objects of ancient Ireland are shown here, starting with the Celtic invaders who landed in the south-west in about 350 B.C. The early kings ruled vast domains like Munster from hill-forts (as at Temuir Emain); a notable war pitted Queen Medb of Connacht against the Ulster hero Cú Chulainn. By the third century A.D., the Connacht kings had expanded and moved to Tara, in Meath; associated with Tara is the legend of Diarmaid and Gráinne. A Tara ruler was Niall of the Nine Hostages, who invaded England in about A.D. 400. A century later a northern King, Fergus MacErc, took lands in Scotland. After Saint Patrick introduced Christianity into Ireland, many wooden churches were constructed; the monastic idea, as brought by Saints Enda and Finnian and disseminated by Saint Columba and others, resulted in monasteries which became centres of learning. Ireland's early culture culminated in the artistic objects labelled on the map.

SCOTLAND

Iona
St. Columba
Fergus MacErc

Cardonagh Stone Cross

Moville
Derry
Antrim
Antiphonary of Bangor
ATLANTIC OCEAN
Raphoe
Catach of St. Columba
ULSTER
Bangor
Candida Casa
Cú Chulainn
Emain Macha
Nendrum
St. Enda
Killala
Lough Erne Reliquiary
Armagh
Downpatrick
Isle of Man
Aghagower
Medb, Queen of Connacht
Monasterboice High Cross
Cruachain
Book of Kells
Tara Brooch
IRISH SEA
Elphin
Athlone Plaque
Tuam
MEATH
Tara
Aran
Clonmacnois High Cross
Clonfert
Clonard
CONNACHT
Diarmaid & Gráinne
Killossy
Glendalough Round Tower
Kildare
Cashel Round Tower
Dinn Rig
LEINSTER
Niall of the Nine Hostages
Ardagh Chalice
Cashel
Aghade
Celtic Invaders
Temuir Emain
Ossory
Ferns
MUNSTER
Ahenny Stone Cross
Lismore
St. Finnian
St. David's
Muskerry
WALES

were allowed to go into exile in France and Spain, but several thousand civilians, including women and girls, were shipped as slaves to the West Indies and Virginia. It was estimated that these deportations and the 11 years of fighting and pillaging reduced the population of Ireland from 1,466,000 to 616,000.

BUT one of Cromwell's most incredibly inhuman punishments was yet to come in the terms of his peace-settlement: almost every Irish landowner and landholding tenant east and south of the River Shannon was forced by law to give up his property and move to the less fertile, rocky and mountainous province of Connaught, or to County Clare on the west side of the river. When Cromwell was finished, Irish Catholics retained only a quarter of all the land in Ireland.

In 1685 the exhausted Irish felt a new and exciting surge of hope. A Catholic King, James II, came to the British throne, and he placed an Irish Catholic, Richard Talbot, the Earl of Tyrconnell, in command of the army in Ireland, which became staffed with Catholic officers. The law against allowing Catholics to hold legal and civic offices was suspended, and judges of the Roman faith began to preside over the courts.

But just as the Crown began to restore land to Catholic owners, James Stuart broke with his Tory supporters in London and was replaced by a Protestant King, William III, the Prince of Orange. James fled to France and then to Ireland, seeking the support of Tyrconnell's Catholic army. William followed with an army of 36,000 for the final clash with James at the Battle of the Boyne in 1690. Naturally the English Protestant and Scottish Presbyterian colonists of the Ulster Plantation came to his aid.

Just as naturally the Catholic Irish backed James, and when he retreated in defeat from the Boyne, the hope for a peaceful Catholic Ireland went with him. When the war dragged to an end at Limerick a year later, there was another great exodus of Irish soldiers to the Continent. This was celebrated in Irish songs and poetry as "The Flight of the Wild Geese".

Now Ireland seemed to be crushed into complete submission, with its leaders gone and its people facing a long and dark century of suppression under the Penal Laws, enacted in vengeance for the Catholic opposition to William. These laws, which were not entirely repealed until 1829, aimed to make the Irish Catholics "insignificant slaves, fit for nothing but to hew wood and draw water". The Anglo-Irish statesman Edmund Burke described their provisions as "a machine . . . as well fitted for the oppression, impoverishment and degradation of a people, and the debasement in them of human nature itself, as ever proceeded from the perverted ingenuity of man".

THE earlier Kilkenny statutes had not been based on religious discrimination. In medieval Ireland both the British colonists and the natives had been Catholics. The Penal Laws assumed, on the other hand, that every Catholic was an enemy outlaw, regardless of wealth or rank or English lineage, and reduced virtually all Irish of the Roman faith—the great majority of the population—to poverty with no rights of citizenship.

Catholics were forbidden to vote or to hold office and were barred from military and civil service, the legal profession and teaching. No Catholic schools were permitted and children were allowed to attend only Protestant schools. A Catholic was not even entitled to own a horse valued at more than five pounds; if a good horse, worth more, were found in his possession, a Protestant could take it from him and force him to accept five pounds as legal payment. Religious rights were severely restricted. Only those few priests who were willing to forswear allegiance to James and the Stuart line were permitted to conduct services. Masses were said secretly in the fields and private homes, with a few men standing guard to watch for British patrols.

Estates owned by Catholics were broken up and confiscated as further penalties for the support given to James II. One of the Penal Laws prohibited a Catholic from leaving all of his land to one son; it had to be divided equally among all of his sons. This meant that a small farm was often broken into five or six tiny tracts, useless for supporting a family.

And so dawned the glorious Georgian 18th century in Ireland, with a handful of newly rich Protestant landowners in the so-called Anglo-Irish ascendancy building gorgeous castles in the country and mansions in Dublin. Meanwhile the Catholic majority, thousands of farming families, lived in near-starvation on potatoes. Jonathan Swift, the dean of Dublin's Anglican Saint Patrick's Cathedral, became so enraged by the plight of the Irish people that he urged them to burn everything from Britain except its coal, and wrote his famous "A Modest Proposal", a savage essay suggesting that Irish children could be fattened up and served on English tables. An anonymous street song came to be sung as Ireland's national anthem:

Oh, Paddy dear, and did ye hear the news
    that's goin' round?
The shamrock is by law forbid to grow
    on Irish ground.
No more Saint Patrick's Day we'll keep,
    his colour can't be seen,
For there's a cruel law ag'in the Wearin'
    o' the Green . . .

Treated as criminal outlaws, the Irish Catholics began to resort to criminal acts of revenge, organizing secret armed bands with such names as the White Boys and the Cork Boys. They prowled the country at night, lynching Protestant land agents and new tenants who had replaced evicted Catholic farmers, burning stables and tearing down fences. Armed groups called houghers hamstrung or massacred sheep and cattle to warn against continued evictions; other bands of men raped, kidnapped and held girls and women for ransom.

One section of the Penal Laws backfired on the British. Ruinous restrictions on Irish industry and tithes for the support of the Anglican Church sorely chafed the Scots-Irish Presbyterian manufacturers of Ulster. The earliest wholesale emigrations of Irish to America in the 18th century were from the North. The Scots-Irish, seeking political freedom from Britain, played a major role in the American Revolution. Among them was General Andrew Jackson, whose parents were born in County Antrim. Four signatories of the Declaration of Independence were born in Ireland and five others were of Irish descent.

News of the American revolt and the French Revolution in 1789 stirred up a strong spirit of agitation in Ulster. When Theobald Wolfe Tone, a young Protestant lawyer, formed the Society of United Irishmen in 1791 ("to abolish all unnatural religious distinctions, to unite all Irishmen against the unjust influence of Great Britain . . ."), that movement's first headquarters was in Belfast. Alarmed by this rumbling, the Government passed a Catholic relief act in 1793, allowing those Catholics who owned land worth 40 shillings or more to hold some voting rights and minor civil-service jobs and to have educational privileges. They were still barred, however, from membership in the Irish Parliament.

That same year, France went to war with Britain. Tone, with the backing of an estimated 150,000 United Irishmen, persuaded the French to support him in a war of insurrection. Wearing the uniform of a French general, he sailed from Brest to Bantry Bay in 1796 with a French fleet carrying a force of 15,000 soldiers. But the admirals in command of the warships were easily discouraged by stormy weather and turned back from the Irish coast without landing.

THE United Irishmen staged a disorganized uprising by themselves in 1798 which was put down by troops under the command of the same Lord Cornwallis who had surrendered earlier to George Washington at the battle of Yorktown. Tone came again, too late, with another French contingent; this time he was captured. Instead of being executed before a firing-squad, as he requested, he was sentenced to be hanged like a common criminal, and so he committed suicide in a British prison cell.

Tone was followed in 1803 by the gallant Robert Emmet, too dreamily idealistic to be a successful revolutionary; his planned outbreak ended in failure. As the historian Edmund Curtis notes in *A History of Ireland*, however, the execution of Emmet and his memorable courtroom speech had a greater impact on the Irish than any act of Parliament or political event. Emmet cried from the dock: "When my country takes her place among the nations of the earth, then, and not till then, let my epitaph be written." Every Irish revolt from then on was launched with the fervent hope that it would write Emmet's epitaph.

EVEN before the uprising of 1798, William Pitt, the British Prime Minister, had decided that the only way Ireland could be kept under British control would be to enact an Act of Union, transferring legislative control of the country from Dublin to the British Parliament at Westminster, and merging the Irish economy into that of Britain. Ireland, in other words, was to cease its existence as a national entity and was to become, like Wales and Scotland, a part of the United Kingdom.

The Act of Union was fought vigorously in the Irish Parliament, not only by such patriots as Henry Grattan but by the Protestants of the Anglo-Irish ascendancy, who controlled the economy and who were not anxious to pay British taxes. Grattan's last plea is highly esteemed by the oratory-loving Irish: "Yet I do not give up my country," he said. "I see her in a swoon but she is not dead; though in her tomb she lies helpless and motionless, still on her lips is the spirit of life and on her cheeks the glow of beauty."

But Pitt passed the act in 1800, buying votes with £1,260,000 in cash and with 48 new or promoted titles in the Irish peerage—one of the most shameful political bribery transactions in history. One of the promises that he made to obtain passage was that Catholics would be included among the Irish representatives seated in the British Houses of Parliament.

Pitt did put this proposal before George III, but the obstinate King turned it down. The Penal Law against representation for the millions of Irish Catholics was not repealed until 1829, when Daniel O'Connell won his hard fight for his people's legislative emancipation.

The most colourful personality in modern Irish history, O'Connell was a charming and gifted Kerryman who gave up a brilliant career in the law in order to serve as a champion of the Irish peasants. He had a special talent for arousing great mass-meetings of tens of thousands with dazzling oratory. His powerful voice could be heard at the outside edges of the huge crowds. He climaxed his battle for emancipation by winning an election to the House of Commons at Clare in 1828 in defiance of the Penal Laws.

As a Catholic, O'Connell could not take his parliamentary seat, of course, but his show of strength forced the British Government to grant almost complete recognition of Catholic rights a year later. When he joined the House, O'Connell supported the Whigs against the Tories in return for favours to Ireland. His critics claimed that he was often taken in by the Whig Government, which did nothing to relieve the oppression of O'Connell's peasant supporters by absentee British landlords. The Emancipation Act, in fact, deprived small Irish farmers of the right to vote; only the larger Catholic property-holders retained the franchise.

WHEN the Whigs went out of office in 1841, O'Connell was already campaigning for repeal of the Act of Union. He insisted on trying to win this difficult objective by peaceful means; he abhorred any display of violence that might cause bloodshed. After rallying all Ireland to his support, he planned a giant mass-demonstration for repeal of the Act of Union on the battlefield at Clontarf, where Brian Boru had defeated the Danes in 1014.

The day before the mass-meeting, which thousands of Irish were ready to attend, the British Government ordered its cancellation and threatened to break it up by armed force if the order was disobeyed. O'Connell called off the meeting. That ended his political career. His disappointed followers turned away from him, and he died a few years later, broken in health and spirit.

The defeat of O'Connell's unfulfilled effort to win repeal of the Act of Union was followed two years later, in 1845, by the worst calamity ever to hit Ireland—the famine caused by the potato blight, which destroyed for three years the crop that more than half the people depended on for food.

THE disaster of the famine killed a million and a half Irish people and forced another million to emigrate from the country between 1846 and 1851. Such starvation arose because poverty-stricken masses of rural people, with no money to buy food, had been reduced to eating nothing except potatoes, which could be grown for a few pennies on a small plot of land. Even before the blight ruined the potatoes, the Irish peasants had been plagued by hunger in the summer months, when the previous year's crop was eaten and new plants had not yet produced food.

Land to grow potatoes on was scarce and difficult to rent; it was more profitable for a large landowner—usually a wealthy man who lived in England—to raise cattle for export than to grow crops.

The British Government did little to relieve the suffering caused by the blight. Beef, pork, lamb and grain raised in Ireland were sold for export, as usual. A small farmer with six children to feed still had to sell his wheat or oats in order to pay his rent while his family went hungry. Otherwise he would be evicted.

Turning Ireland's food products over to famine sufferers instead of letting them go to market, or stopping rents or evictions as an emergency relief measure, seemed inconceivable to the British officials of that time. As Cecil Woodham-Smith points out in her definitive study of the famine, *The Great Hunger*, the British believed religiously in the *laissez faire* theory of economics; a government must never interfere with private commerce or with the rights of a landlord to make a profit and evict a tenant.

By the same token, the Government itself did not wish to compete with private trade by buying and distributing food. When the Prime Minister, Robert Peel, took the drastic step of buying American corn for distribution in Ireland, he did so with the utmost secrecy. When the Government was finally faced with providing emergency soup kitchens and large-scale food-dispensing centres in Ireland, nobody except a few Army ordnance officers knew how to handle the task.

Being unprepared ideologically or otherwise to cope with the problem, the British could provide little help for Ireland. The Irish could only feel that they were being left to starve to death; the British, the accusation ran, were using the famine to carry on the work of Cromwell.

IN the same mood of bitterness which prevailed long after the famine years, the Irish rallied behind a new leader, Charles Stewart Parnell, who carried on the banner of Home Rule that had slipped from Dan O'Connell's hands. Parnell was a Protestant landowner, but he rose to prominence and popularity in Ireland as a dedicated defender of small farmers suffering from landlord exploitation. He went on to greater fame and power as leader of the Irish faction in the House of Commons.

But in 1890, when Parnell was at the crest of his prestige and influence, he was named corespondent in a divorce case brought by William O'Shea, one of his political followers, against his wife Kitty. Parnell never denied the charge, and after Mrs. O'Shea was divorced he married her. At another time in another country, such a scandal might have been overlooked, but in the Victorian era and in severely moral Ireland, it meant that Parnell's career was finished. The majority of Parnell's supporters deserted their fallen chief. The cause of Home Rule had been dealt a staggering blow. The Irish could hope only for better luck in the approaching 20th century.

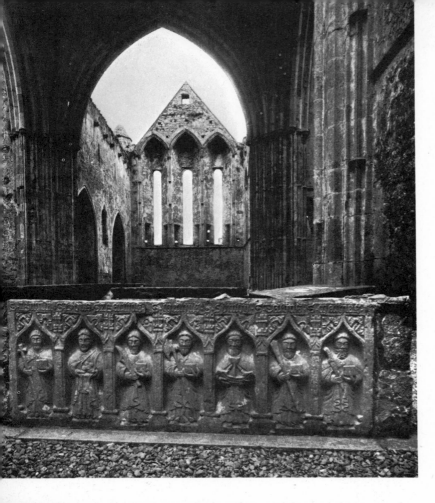

Undying Echoes of a Heroic Past

Long before Europe's Middle Ages, Ireland was a centre of artistic and intellectual excellence. Barely a century after Saint Patrick introduced the Christian faith, Irish missionaries were travelling to Britain and the Continent. If the sixth century was a time of flourishing monasteries, the seventh opened the Golden Age of Art. With new motifs from Europe and new techniques, Irish craftsmen achieved a peak of sophisticated ornamentation in metal-work and manuscripts. This resplendent period was interrupted by the raids of barbarous Scandinavians in the late eighth century. During the era of England's domination, the memory of Ireland's religious, political and cultural freedom comforted the soul of an oppressed people.

A SUPERB SANCTUARY, the small Cormac's Chapel at Cashel is decorated by a Romanesque doorway. The most remarkable building of the 12th century, it has a wealth of carving and ornamentation.

IMPOSING STRUCTURES crown the Rock of Cashel (*opposite*), which was until 1101 a seat of Munster kings. The cathedral (*right*), Saint Patrick's Cross (*left*) and the Round Tower (*centre*) dominate the hill.

FOREIGN DOMINANCE *ended the Golden Age and caused centuries of pain*

THE MASSACRE OF DROGHEDA, a County Louth city, was staged in 1649 by Oliver Cromwell, shown to the left above mounted on a white charger. Seeking to avenge English deaths in Ulster, Cromwell killed 3,500 people, soldiers and townspeople, opening a period of oppression lasting for 30 years.

THE BATTLE OF THE BOYNE, won by William III of Orange in 1690 (*below*), dashed Irish hopes for Roman Catholic rule. Just as the Catholic King of England James II was restoring rights to the Irish, the Protestant William (*centre*) replaced him, defeated him at Boyne, and crushed the Irish rebels.

FAMINE killed more than a million people in the late 1840s when a fungus blight attacked the potato crop and destroyed it

SEVERE STARVATION caused so many deaths that corpses were piled on carts (*above*) and buried without coffins. Although some food and money came from English and Irish charities, poor communication prevented effective distribution of relief.

THE DEVASTATING BLIGHT in 1845 destroyed the food which over half the Irish ate exclusively, the potato. Peasants like this mother and son dug in stubble fields looking for undiseased plants. The fungus attacked again in 1846 and 1848.

A MASS PROTEST against shortage of rations brought starving families to storm government workhouses, which sheltered the needy. With the workhouses full, the government instituted a relief programme, but in the crisis the system collapsed.

FORCED EVICTION drove tenants from their homes (*below*). In order to keep the evicted from returning, landlords got the local sheriff (*on horseback*) to raze, or "tumble", the cottages. The cleared area was subsequently changed into pasture land.

MASS EMIGRATION from Ireland to America occurred during the famine years. From 1847 to 1855 more than a million emigrants bade farewell to their relatives remaining behind and boarded decrepit cargo ships bound for the United States.

Soldiers survey the gutted interior of Dublin's General Post Office, virtually demolished by British shell-fire during the unsuccessful

1916 Easter Week rising which led to the Anglo-Irish war.

4

The
Troubles

THE Irish are quick to admit their no-
toriety for fighting among themselves. A
woman in Athlone was talking recently to an
American about the unanimously warm wel-
come given to President Kennedy when he visited her country in 1963. "It was the first time
everybody in Ireland agreed on anything since
the British tried to put through conscription in
1918," she said.

That earlier agreement among the contrary
Irish minds in the closing months of World War
I was an ominous one. Centuries of oppression
and cruelty had haunted Ireland; now the nation was to experience an outburst of violence
rivalling any of the savagery of the past. The
country was well aware at the war's end that
thousands of volunteers had already given service with the British Army in France. It was
seething with indignation over the execution of
15 leaders of the 1916 Easter Week rebellion
in Dublin. In a gesture of defiance towards the
British, the surviving senior officer of that brief

uprising, Eamon de Valera, had just been elected in County Clare to Daniel O'Connell's old seat in the British Parliament. John Dillon, head of the Irish delegation in the House of Commons, warned the British Prime Minister, David Lloyd George, that forcing compulsory military service on the Irish might be the last straw.

Lloyd George nevertheless pushed the Irish Conscription Bill through Parliament. In outrage, all Ireland's divided political factions rose together against Britain. A few months after the armistice, when de Valera's Sinn Fein movement declared Ireland's independence and started an armed revolt, the whole country, except for four pro-British counties in Ulster, was united behind it.

THE earlier Easter Week rebellion of 1916, which began the series of events that culminated in the winning of Irish independence, had had no such popular support at its inception. Since the fall of Parnell in 1890, the Irish Home Rule movement had broken into several conservative and radical groups. Eventually there were at least 15 active revolutionary groups. None of them possessed a large following; all were divided within their own ranks.

The extreme nationalist faction, for example, was made up of an alliance between the Sinn Fein (Ourselves Alone) party, under the leadership of Arthur Griffith, and the Irish Republican Brotherhood, headed by Tom Clarke, who had spent 15 years as a political prisoner in an English jail. Clarke wanted an independent Irish republic, as did most of the Sinn Feiners. Griffith favoured a monarchy, with the English monarch holding two separate roles—King of England and King of Ireland—and separate British and Irish parliamentary governments.

The nationalist factions had come close to starting an armed war against the violently anti-Home Rule and anti-Catholic unionists of Ulster shortly before the outbreak of World War I. The Ulster Irish, led by Edward Carson, were Presbyterians and Anglicans. They were violently opposed to Home Rule because they refused to be governed by Catholics in Dublin.

When the British Government offered Ireland a mild form of Home Rule in 1910 ("full self-government in regard to purely Irish affairs"), Carson threatened to set up a separate Ulster government by armed force. He openly ran guns into the North and in 1912 organized the Ulster Volunteers, a military auxiliary. Carson was backed by the generals of the British Army's occupation troops in Ireland, who warned the Government that they would not suppress a revolt in Ulster.

THE Irish nationalists hastened to form their own military organizations, too, smuggling guns into the country and drilling troops in preparation for a fight against Carson. The Irish Republican Brotherhood and a few Sinn Feiners organized the soldiers of the Irish Volunteers. One of the first recruits to sign up was Eamon de Valera, a serious young teacher of mathematics. The Labour party in Dublin established the Irish Citizen Army, hailed by Lenin as the first Communist army in Europe. It was commanded by the fiery James Connolly and its secretary was Sean O'Casey, not yet a famous dramatist.

When Britain went to war against Germany in 1914, many of the Irish Volunteers, the military arm of Sinn Fein, enlisted in the British Army. Carson's Ulster Volunteers joined the British Army as a unit. A grateful Parliament promised to do nothing about Home Rule until the war ended. Now free from the threat of attack from the North, the Irish rebels began to make other plans for their Volunteer and Citizen Army soldiers, who were drilling and marching in public with rifles on their shoulders. One day, under the eyes of British officers, the Volunteer troops even staged a sham attack on the Dublin Post Office.

The citizen-soldiers claimed that they served "neither King George not the Kaiser, but Ireland". Yet all of them believed in the old slogan of Gaelic insurrectionaries, "England's misfortune is Ireland's opportunity". Irish sympathizers in New York and Sir Roger Casement, an Irish agent in Germany, sought arms and ammunition from the Germans. The Volunteers and the Citizen Army joined forces and plotted the capture of Dublin. The date set was Monday of Easter Week, 1916, when most of the officers in the British military garrisons would be out of town attending the races at Fairyhouse.

The rebellion was doomed before its start by hasty and poorly co-ordinated planning and the inadequate strength of the Irish forces. Eoin MacNeill, chief of the Volunteers, was opposed to staging an armed revolt while England was at war, and the other leaders did not let him know of their plans until the last minute. Furious, he ordered the attack to be called off.

The plotters decided to go on with the uprising. Most of their followers did not hear until too late that MacNeill's order had been counter-manded. In several provincial cities where attacks were to be launched at the same time as the assault on Dublin, nothing happened. The men reporting for action on Monday morning in Dublin numbered only around 1,200 instead of the 2,400 that were expected.

Through another mix-up in messages the *Aud*, a German ship carrying arms for the uprising, reached Tralee Bay in Kerry three days before her scheduled arrival. Trying to head her off, Sir Roger Casement raced to Tralee by submarine but arrived too late. The *Aud* was surrounded by the British and blown up by its crew. After rowing ashore in a small boat, Casement was arrested by local police and was later hanged in London for treason.

DESPITE these confusions, the small contingent of rebels captured several key points in Dublin on Monday, and established a provisional Irish Republic Government headquarters at the Post Office, hoisting a green, white and orange Irish flag on the roof of the building. Patrick Pearse, commander of this new Irish Republican Army, read on the Post Office steps the now-famous proclamation that begins: "Irishmen and Irishwomen: In the name of God and of the dead generations from which she receives her old tradition of nationhood,

MAJOR GROUPS IN THE REVOLUTION

SINN FEIN: Organized as a political party in 1904, Sinn Fein (Ourselves Alone) demanded the political and cultural independence of all of Ireland.

IRISH REPUBLICAN BROTHERHOOD: An offshoot of Sinn Fein, the I.R.B. wanted independence for Ireland, but favoured continued alliance with Britain.

IRISH VOLUNTEERS: A military group organized by members of the I.R.B. and Sinn Fein, it began the Easter Week uprising of 1916.

IRISH REPUBLICAN ARMY: The Irish Volunteers became the I.R.A. when the independence of Ireland was proclaimed during the Easter Week uprising.

ULSTER VOLUNTEERS: Organized by Ulster Irishmen who opposed independence, this military group enlisted in the British Army in World War I.

IRISH CITIZEN ARMY: This group was the military auxiliary of the Irish Labour party, which demanded immediate and total independence.

FIANNA FAIL: A political party, Fianna Fail (Warriors of Destiny) was opposed to the partition of Ulster from Southern Ireland.

BRITISH FORCES: Troops attempting to put down the rebellion of 1918-21 were divided into three groups: the Royal Irish Constabulary; the *élite* Auxiliaries, an organization of former British officers who had served in World War I; and the Black and Tans, a force of former British enlisted men.

Ireland, through us, summons her children to her flag and strikes for her freedom."

The British, taken by surprise, rushed troops into the city and pinned down the rebels under heavy machine-gun and artillery fire. A gunboat on the River Liffey demolished most of the buildings on O'Connell Street, and the Post Office was burnt. After holding out all week, the Irish were finally forced to surrender on the Saturday.

In the fighting, 56 Republican soldiers and 216 Dublin civilians were killed or died from wounds. The British reported 130 dead.

This opening battle of the revolution stirred many Irish deeply, but most of Ireland viewed the destruction and bloodshed with glum indifference or irritation, regarding the whole performance as a reckless and unnecessary outburst by a few hot-headed political fanatics. Easter Week sparked no patriotic feeling in the many Irish families who had sons fighting with British forces in the trenches in France.

Then the British authorities began to put the leaders of the rebellion to death, sending three or four of them at a time before firing-squads after quick and secret court martials. James Connolly, badly wounded at the Post Office, was carried to the execution yard on a stretcher and propped up before the firing-squad in a chair.

The results were immediate. The Irish people stiffened in anger. Annoyed embarrassment was swept away by a fierce and choking flush of national pride. The Catholic bishop of Limerick, Edward Thomas O'Dwyer, denounced the British general, Sir John Maxwell, who had ordered the executions: "Personally I regard your action with horror and I believe that it has outraged the conscience of the country."

Pictures of the executed rebels were hung on cottage walls beside those of Robert Emmet and the Sacred Heart of Jesus. The spirit of revolution that the Easter Week men had failed to inspire in their march on Dublin had been aroused by their deaths in the prison yard. The stage was set for the next and final fight for freedom in 1918.

LEADERSHIP in the Sinn Fein movement was now more or less thrust upon de Valera; all the other chiefs except Arthur Griffith were dead, and Griffith, never a militant Republican, had not fought in Easter Week. De Valera had distinguished himself in that action, commanding a small Volunteer detachment. He had been sentenced to death with the other leaders but his sentence had been suspended and he was imprisoned in England.

There he found himself heading the surviving die-hard Republicans. After Easter Week, known and suspected rebels from all over Ireland were rounded up and shipped with the surrendered Dublin insurgents to jails and internment camps in Britain, where they turned to de Valera for guidance. A distant and stern man, with no warm small-talk, he was nevertheless trusted and deeply respected. One of his fellow-prisoners at Dartmoor and Lewes recalls: "He became the leader of us all without any consultation, debate or election. Whenever any proposal was made or discussed, the first question everyone asked was: 'What does Dev think of it?' "

The political prisoners, numbering more than 2,500, were too much for the British authorities to handle. They were released, some late in 1916 and the rest in 1917, and welcomed in Ireland with wildly enthusiastic torchlight parades.

WHEN de Valera was let out of the gates of Pentonville jail in England, he was handed a telegram telling him that he had been nominated as the Sinn Fein candidate in an East Clare by-election for a vacant seat in the House of Commons. No one could serve in the Commons without taking an oath of allegiance to the King, which the Sinn Feiners refused to do. But that did not stop them from entering election contests to show their popular support and to discredit the rival Irish Parliamentary party, which favoured moderate Home Rule with continued membership in the British Empire.

Sinn Fein had now become an out-and-out movement for the establishment of an Irish republic. De Valera's candidacy in East Clare was watched by all Ireland and Britain as a crucial test of Sinn Fein strength.

De Valera opened his campaign by reading the Republican manifesto that Pearse had spoken on the Post Office steps in Dublin. That, he said, was what he stood for. His Parliamentary party opponent pleaded against having Irishmen "shot down in a futile and insane attempt to establish an Irish Republic". De Valera won the election with a 2 to 1 majority.

The line was now clearly drawn, but the British were in no mood to give up Ireland while they were fighting a war. Eighty-four Republicans were arrested in the following month.

Officially installed as the Sinn Fein leader, with the support of Arthur Griffith, the party's founder, de Valera denied pro-German sympathy and discouraged armed violence against the British for the duration of the war. In 1918, when Lloyd George as Prime Minister aroused bitterness with his plan for conscription, most of the Sinn Feiners were eager for another Easter Week uprising. De Valera had difficulty persuading them to maintain what he called "passive resistance". They called a general strike instead, stopping all transport and all work for one day of protest in every city except Belfast.

Robert Brennan, one of de Valera's aides, recalls that during the conscription uproar a young man pedalled his bicycle 45 miles one day from a town in County Offaly to the Sinn Fein headquarters in Dublin, carrying an empty canvas sack.

"We had a meeting last night," he said, "and we decided to meet the menace of conscription by passive resistance, so they sent me in to pick up a bag of bombs."

In April 1918, when Sinn Fein campaigns to prevent conscription were being organized, the police captured an Irish agent who had been landed from a German submarine on the Galway coast. The British Government claimed that he had been arranging a conspiracy between the Germans and Sinn Fein, and immediately deported de Valera and 73 other Sinn Fein leaders, without trials, to prisons in England.

DE VALERA and most of these party chiefs were still in prison when the war ended. But the I.R.A. had one dedicated and highly skilled leader still at large, a husky, handsome man named Michael Collins. In January 1919, when the Sinn Fein convened the first meeting of Dail Eireann, the Irish rebel Parliament, and declared the independence of the Irish Republic, Collins was only 29 years old. He had, however, already spent two years organizing intelligence networks and combat units. Collins seemed fearless; while the British were offering £10,000 for his arrest, he rode his bicycle calmly through the Dublin streets with a revolver in his pocket.

For all his charm, Collins was a completely ruthless terrorist. His squad of gunmen in trench-coats and slouch hats killed 14 secret agents of the British in Dublin on November 21,

1920, a day afterwards known as Bloody Sunday. Most of the victims were shot in their beds or getting out of bed to answer a knock on the door. One agent's wife tried to shield her husband while he was climbing out a window. Collins's men dragged her away and fired seven shots into her husband, leaving him dead and hanging half-way out the window.

That afternoon the British soldiers and police surrounded Croke Park, where a big crowd was watching a Dublin–Tipperary football match. The official plan was to close the exits and search the crowd for hidden weapons, but a group of soldiers opened fire. One player and 11 spectators were killed and many others injured. Thirty revolvers were dropped on the ground by frantically running spectators.

EARLIER, in February 1919, Collins had designed a plan that enabled de Valera to escape from Lincoln jail, sending him a cake with a key to his cell door concealed inside it. But during the revolution of the next three years, which the Irish refer to with quiet understatement as The Troubles, it was Collins, rather than de Valera, who directed the Republican Army. As President of the Government of resistance, de Valera was more concerned with policy than with fighting, and he spent a year and a half in the United States trying to win American support and money for his cause.

The Big Fellow, as Collins was called, fought an evasive hit-and-run war. He avoided pitched battles like that of Easter Week. The I.R.A. seldom numbered as many as 15,000 men, all untrained civilians, poorly armed and with few motor vehicles. They faced a combined British Army and constabulary of more than 70,000 mobile troops. Collins divided his men into tactical units, which he referred to as flying columns, each with 75 to 100 men, and often with fewer than that.

A flying column was usually assembled for a quick raid on a police barracks or for an ambush on a convoy of British troops on a lonely rural road. After the attack the force would disperse and scatter into the fields or bogs. The next morning some of the I.R.A. men would be working innocently at their jobs as farmers, teachers or shopkeepers; others would go into hiding until the next assignment.

These small harassments wore down the British more effectively than might be imagined. They were carried out relentlessly and incessantly all over Ireland; the authorities could never be sure when or where the I.R.A. would strike next.

BEWILDERED by the invisible enemy, the British could do little more than impose early curfews, search homes in the hope of finding a suspect and carry out harsh acts of reprisal. Erskine Childers, an English convert to the Irish crusade, wrote in 1920 for a London newspaper this description of Dublin in the curfew hours: "As the citizens go to bed, the barracks spring to life. Lorries, tanks, and armoured searchlight cars muster in fleets. . . . Think of raiding a private house at dead of night in a tank. . . . A thunder of knocks; no time to dress (even for a woman alone) or the door will crash in. On opening, in charge the soldiers—literally charge—with fixed bayonets and in full war-kit. . . . Imagine the moral effect of such a procedure on the young officers and men told off for this duty! Is it any wonder that gross abuses occur: looting, wanton destruction, brutal severity to women?"

The British were reluctant to assign these Gestapo-type raids to Army units because the Government denied that a state of war existed in Ireland. The task of coping with the I.R.A. was left mainly to the police force of the Royal Irish Constabulary—enlarged for the emergency with two special temporary-duty groups, each with 15,000 tough veterans of World War I recruited in England and Scotland through newspaper advertisements offering "rough and dangerous" military service in Ireland.

These two special groups, filled with irresponsible and hard-drinking youngsters just out of the trenches, were the Black and Tans and the Auxiliary Cadets, an *élite* corps consisting only of ex-officers. The Black and Tans, so-called because of their makeshift uniforms of Irish Constabulary dark green and army khaki, were paid 10 shillings a day. Although they became notorious in the literature and films of The Troubles as brutal and reckless killers, they were actually less feared in Ireland than the better-dressed and supposedly higher-principled pound-a-day Auxiliaries.

The Black and Tans burned and looted such towns as Ennistymon, Lahinch and Trim, but it was the Auxiliaries who set fire to the entire business district of Cork in reprisal for an I.R.A. attack on an Auxiliary patrol earlier the same day. Reinforced by the Black and Tans, they held back at gun-point the firemen who came to the burning buildings. The Auxiliaries were well equipped with trucks and armoured cars and roamed all over the country, committing drunken vandalisms and terrifying old people and children.

The Auxiliary Cadets' commanding officer, General F. P. Crozier, resigned from his post in 1921 because he was unable to maintain discipline. Crozier gave up in disgust after discovering that an Auxiliary officer had ordered his men to capture the outspoken pro-Republican Catholic bishop of Killaloe, Dr. Michael Fogarty, and to drown him in a weighted sack in the River Shannon. Luckily for the bishop, he happened to be out of town on the day that the Auxiliaries came to pick him up.

SENSELESS and sadistic acts of cruelty were frequently practised by the I.R.A. as well as by the Black and Tans and the Auxiliaries. In County Clare a party of rebels buried a British magistrate up to his neck in sand just below the high-tide mark on a seaside beach so that the rising water would slowly cover his face. The next day his tormentors found him still alive. They dug him up and replanted him closer to the incoming waves, again leaving him to watch the tide creep up to his neck and chin. This time the rising waters finished the job.

The single act of the revolution that aroused more world-wide interest and sympathy for Ireland's struggle than any military terrorism was the long hunger-strike of Terence MacSwiney, the Lord Mayor of Cork, after he was imprisoned in England in the autumn of 1920.

A few months earlier, MacSwiney's predecessor as Lord Mayor, Thomas MacCurtain, who was also the commander of the Cork Brigade of the I.R.A., had been shot in his home by British police. When MacSwiney replaced the murdered mayor he also assumed his I.R.A. duties. He was conducting an Army meeting in City Hall when he was arrested and charged with possessing documents "likely to cause disaffection to His Majesty".

MACSWINEY claimed that citizens of the Irish Republic could be tried only in Republican courts—which the Sinn Fein Government was then operating in 27 counties. In protest against the infringement of his and others' legal rights, he said, he would refuse food while in jail. Ten other I.R.A. men arrested with him also began a hunger-strike. After 70 days of fasting, MacSwiney was still alive, and many British and American people who had paid little attention to the revolution in Ireland up to that time were following the daily reports on his condition with growing compassion. MacSwiney died on October 24, 1920, his 74th day on the hunger-strike. Two other prisoners died at the same time.

A guard of honour of uniformed I.R.A. soldiers and a procession of thousands of Irish marched behind MacSwiney's Irish-flag-draped coffin when it was taken through the streets of London before being shipped to Cork. Not a sound of protest was heard from the crowds of respectfully silent British spectators.

In 1921, the third year of the revolt, the Republican Army and the Irish people were still far from subdued and the British authorities were preparing to launch what Winston Churchill called "the most unlimited exercise of rough-handed force".

But before the British could undertake drastic measures, King George V intervened with a public plea for a peaceful settlement. A few days later de Valera received an invitation to confer with the Prime Minister, Lloyd George. A truce was called.

The big stumbling-block in the peace-treaty talks which followed was the question of the six north-eastern Ulster counties, which had shortly before been partitioned from the rest of Ireland as a province of the United Kingdom with its own parliamentary government. De Valera was willing to compromise on his earlier demand for an Irish republic and accept membership in the British Commonwealth, but he flatly refused continuation of partition.

De Valera, however, was not present at the treaty conference-table; he remained in Dublin while other rebel leaders represented Ireland at the talks in London. The Irish delegates were finally convinced that a refusal of the Prime Minister's demand for the partition would cause all-out war. Without de Valera's approval, they signed a treaty agreeing to partition.

Some enraged I.R.A. leaders wanted to arrest the delegates and charge them with treason when they returned to Dublin. But most of the Irish people and the Catholic hierarchy were anxious for peaceful settlement. Over the strong opposition of de Valera and his Republican diehards, the treaty was approved by the Dail on January 7, 1922. Ireland was made a free state in the British Commonwealth. The six Ulster counties remained a province of the United Kingdom.

But the achievement of limited independence did not bring peace to Ireland. As soon as British troops were withdrawn from the land, a bitter civil war broke out between the pro-treaty Free State Government, headed by Collins and Griffith, and de Valera's Republicans.

THE first shots were fired on the morning of June 28 in the centre of Dublin. Free Staters, using borrowed British artillery, mounted a bombardment on the historic Four Courts building, fortified as a Republican stronghold. As in the Easter Week battle, the fighting went on for eight days. Sixty men were killed and 300 wounded. While the Republicans were making a desperate last stand de Valera, who had rejoined his old I.R.A. unit, managed to escape from the city. Most of his soldiers were taken prisoner.

The loss of Dublin doomed the Republicans but the war dragged on for another year in the hills and small towns of the south and west. On August 12, Griffith died suddenly from strain and overwork, and 10 days later Collins was killed in a small skirmish on a country road in Cork. William Cosgrave took over the leadership of the Free State Government and refused a peace settlement offered by de Valera. When the Republicans abandoned the war on April 30, 1923, de Valera and the I.R.A. chiefs were forced to go into hiding.

Four months later Cosgrave called for a general election to strengthen his Government's position. From hiding, de Valera announced his candidacy for the Dail from his old constituency in Clare and declared that he would campaign in person. When he appeared at a rally in Ennis to make his opening campaign speech, he was arrested by Free State troops and imprisoned for almost a year. While in prison, he was elected in Clare, receiving twice as many votes as Eoin MacNeill, the Cosgrave party's candidate.

DE VALERA remained in jail until a general amnesty bill restored all Republicans to citizenship in 1924. He then broke with Sinn Fein in a dispute over the oath of allegiance to the British Crown, required under the Free State treaty for membership in the Irish Parliament, and formed his own Republican party, Fianna Fail (Warriors of Destiny), which became Cosgrave's strongest opposition.

The de Valera party was still faced, however, with the oath of allegiance problem. It was difficult to see how any political party could survive without representation in the Dail. But to gain a seat in the legislative body, a winning candidate had to swear allegiance to the King on a Bible and sign a statement of loyalty to him.

De Valera found a way round the obstacle by making one of the frequent abstract distinctions that have driven his political rivals to distraction. He decided that his Fianna Fail members would not really be taking the oath if they kept their hands off the Bible and announced while signing the allegiance statement that they were doing so only to gain admission to the Dail.

THUS the anti-oath Fianna Fail began to send members to Parliament and gained the power that eventually enabled de Valera to win control of the Government in 1932. One of his first official moves was to abolish the oath of allegiance. In 1936, after the abdication of King Edward VIII, de Valera and the Dail recognized George VI as head of the British Commonwealth, in which Ireland held membership; they denied him recognition, however, as King of Ireland. Under the new Irish constitution promulgated that year, Ireland was to have a President, elected by the people every seven years as a non-political head of state. The real chief executive became a Prime Minister, elected by a parliamentary majority.

De Valera's party remained in control of the Government continuously in the years after 1932. His one regret during that period was the continued existence of partition. Since the 26 Catholic counties left the Commonwealth in 1949 to become the Republic of Eire, the chances of reunion with Protestant Ulster have seemed remoter than ever. The leadership of Fianna Fail has been passed on to a younger veteran of the old I.R.A., Sean Lemass. In 1959 the Chief, as de Valera's followers call him, became the President of Ireland.

The President's handsome residence, in Dublin's Phoenix Park, was formerly the viceregal palace of the British Governor-General. An Irish taxi-driver explained to one of de Valera's recent visitors that in the days of the governor-generals a cabbie, waiting for a passenger paying a call at the palace, would be served a sandwich and a bottle of ale.

"They don't do it any more, sir," the taxi-driver said. "But of course we are no longer as desperately hungry for a sandwich as we were back in those days when the British were here."

British troops round up rebels in Dublin in 1920 in front of the General Post Office (left), rebuilt after being destroyed in 1916.

Revolution, Civil War, and a Difficult Freedom

Although a yearning for home rule obsessed the Irish for centuries, they did not mount a full-scale rebellion until 1918, when Britain attempted to draft Irish soldiers into the Army. Indignant, Ireland claimed its independence. The next three years ran bloody with the carnage of guerrilla attacks and wholesale killing. In 1921 England granted Ireland self-determination—with conditions. The separation of six Northern counties from the 26 Southern counties was unacceptable to a sizeable minority in the rest of the country. A civil war ensued which lasted for 10 months. After a truce was signed, the nation subsided into torpor. Only in the last few years has an able new Prime Minister, Sean Lemass, been able to awaken Ireland from its exhaustion and begin to orient it towards international industrial society.

LEADERS of the rebellion, seen attending a hurling match in 1921, were (*left to right*) Arthur Griffith, Eamon de Valera, Laurence O'Neill and Michael Collins. Later de Valera broke with Griffith over partition.

BRUTAL REPRISAL was wrought by the English Black and Tans on the little town of Balbriggan on September 20, 1920. To avenge the death of a British soldier, the troops burned 25 houses and a factory to the ground.

A MAGNETIC FIGURE, Constance Countess Markievicz confers with a trade-union leader, Cathal O'Shannon. Born to Irish Protestants and married to a Polish aristocrat, she fought in uniform for Irish independence.

REBELLION *provoked heroic defiance, wholesale reprisals, and the rising grief of a suppressed people*

REPUBLICAN TROOPS are inspected by Eamon de Valera in County Clare. Relying on guerrilla tactics, the Army staged ambushes and surprise attacks on British soldiers, then hid in households loyal to the Republic.

A PATRIOTIC MARTYR, Terence MacSwiney, Lord Mayor of Cork, was given a solemn funeral in 1920. Imprisoned in England for I.R.A. activities, he died after a 74-day hunger strike, exciting world-wide attention.

PROTESTING WOMEN, dressed in deep mourning and saying their rosaries, assembled with 20,000 other Dubliners on March 14, 1921, to pray for six Republican prisoners who were executed that day by the English.

THE LONG-AWAITED TREATY is ratified in Dublin on January 14, 1922, ending the conflict with England and establishing the Irish Free State in the British Commonwealth. Arthur Griffith, with glasses and seated in the middle of the bench at the left centre, was instrumental in negotiating the agreement and in gaining support for it in an Ireland sharply divided on the question.

Demonstrators protest against the imprisonment of Republicans by the Free Staters in 1923. The Republicans opposed partition.

AN ASCETIC HERO of The Troubles, Eamon de Valera was Ireland's Prime Minister for 21 years. He sought to return his nation to self-reliance and the language and customs of the past.

A QUIET PROGRESSIVE, Sean Lemass became Prime Minister in 1959. Though a veteran of the I.R.A., he represents newer ideas and has encouraged industry and foreign investment.

5

Devotion
to the
Church

A N American Communist returned from a tour of Europe a few years ago and reported to a fellow party member in New York the progress of Marxism in the countries that he had visited. He mentioned that Communism in Ireland was forced to operate underground. "The Irish Communists won't identify themselves publicly as members of the party," he explained, "because they're afraid they may be excommunicated by the Catholic Church."

Excommunication is indeed a stigma to be avoided, even by a Communist, in the Republic of Ireland, one of the most solidly Roman Catholic nations in the world. The partition of 1921 segregated most of Ireland's Protestants under British government in the six Northern counties of Ulster and left the area of the Republic with a population, now 2.8 million, that is 95 per cent Catholic.

Although there are some 150,000 Protestants in the Republic, there are large areas where there are no Protestants at all. Many smaller towns have only two or three families in their dwindling Anglican, Presbyterian and Methodist congregations. An Irishman observed recently that Sunday services at the Anglican cathedral in his community, well filled 100 years ago, are now attended by "five

75

maiden ladies proudly hymning their defiance''.

The overwhelming dominance of Catholicism in Ireland leaves little, if any, separation between the Church and the state. As the writer Sean O'Faolain points out in a study of Irish Catholicism, the Church in Ireland does not need to resort to politics as it does in more secularized countries, such as Italy and France; it holds its power simply through the old bond of faith, unbroken in the Irish people since the Middle Ages. The Government, run by devout Catholics, is naturally influenced by the Church, and the average Irishman sees nothing alarming in this—after all, his own family life is also guided by the Church, and those politicians need the priests to keep an eye on them.

THE Irish Constitution guarantees religious freedom to all sects and creeds, but it acknowledges "the special position of the Holy Catholic Apostolic and Roman Church as the guardian of the Faith professed by the great majority of the citizens". The Government, on both the national and local levels, makes few moves affecting social welfare, education or health without the approval of the Catholic hierarchy, and any proposal strongly opposed by the Church would be in serious trouble. The Sinn Fein revolution against the British succeeded partly because it was not opposed by the bishops, and received outspoken support from some of them. The subsequent civil war waged by de Valera's anti-treaty Republicans against the Free State failed partly because the clergy preached against it and denied the sacraments to the rebels.

All public primary education in the country is under religious control—whether it is Catholic, Protestant or even, in a few cases, Jewish. In every Catholic town the national, or public, primary school attended by Catholic children is supervised by the local Catholic parish priest. He selects and hires the principal and approves the appointment of teachers. If nuns, priests or Catholic religious brothers teach in national schools, as they often do, the Government pays them the same salary it gives to lay teachers. Protestant children, however, are not required to attend Catholic-supervised schools. They go to a Government-supported school directed by the local Protestant minister. If there are not enough Protestant families in the community to require such a school, the children are provided with transport to the nearest town that has one. Secondary schools, also subsidized by the Government, are in private hands, with many of the high schools and preparatory schools run by religious orders.

The Government also builds, with the ample funds of its Irish Hospital Sweepstakes lottery, hospitals, mental institutions and homes for the poor and aged which are staffed by members of religious orders. The dominating buildings in every sizeable Irish town are the hospital and the Catholic church, and the dominating figure in local community life is the Catholic priest, "without whom", Sean O'Faolain writes, "any picture of modern Ireland is unthinkable".

The priest is deeply involved, directly or indirectly, in everything in his town, and he is an unofficial clan leader, consulted for advice and guidance not only in matters of family trouble but also in business or legal disputes, arguments over the ownership of livestock or land boundaries and squabbles about the selection of the local football team. In certain aspects of town and county government that concern social life, the priest's word is law. Without his consent, or at least his lack of opposition, it is impossible to open a new dance-hall or pub. It is owing to the Church that Ireland has no night-clubs or strip shows.

YET for all his involvement in community life, and despite the fact that the local church is usually the town's social and recreation centre, the Irish priest is placed on a pedestal that keeps him from mixing intimately and familiarly with his parishioners. Like a general in an army community, he belongs to a special high caste. He is too respected and honoured for his calling to be treated like other men. After he receives Holy Orders, even the members of his own family are in awe of him. It would be hard to imagine an Irish publisher bringing out a novel about an alcoholic priest, like the American writer Edwin O'Connor's *The Edge of Sadness*. Such a public discussion of human weakness in a man of God would be regarded as scandalous.

Members of the clergy in Ireland, in fact, are celebrities whose ecclesiastical ceremonies and public appearances are played up with pictures and headlines in the newspapers like the doings of film or television stars in the United States. An indication of the high esteem for priests in Ireland is the fact that even in the smallest rural parishes the priests obtain their major support from privately paid tithes or a few annual offerings—and not from money obtained by passing collection baskets at Sunday Mass. Unlike Catholic pastors in some other countries, the Irish priest in charge of a larger parish is provided with a rectory where he lives alone, befitting his high station. His curates share another house.

THE public image of the Irish priest has changed considerably in recent years. Although Catholicism in Ireland is still sterner than the more relaxed variety found in Latin countries, the average modern cleric, with an Austin in his garage and a telephone and television set in his rectory, is much more tolerant and broad-minded than the fire-breathing, small-town Irish pastor of 50 years ago. Many an Irishman who was young at the turn of the century has a vivid memory of the village priest hurrying along a road in the evening to chase home with his blackthorn stick the romantic young couple reported to be sitting on a gate. Even the most critical anticlerical Irish agree that those tyrannical guardians of their flocks have faded away with the clay pipe and the jaunting car, and that Ireland today is not the "priest-ridden" country that it used to be.

"The young people now won't stand for iron-handed moral dictatorship and the Irish Church is no longer inclined to exert it," a bishop in the midlands says. "The clergy in a thoroughly Catholic country like this one naturally has more authority than it has elsewhere, but we are well aware that authority can't be as rigid as it was in the time of Queen Victoria."

IRISH Catholics point to a number of recent expressions of public disagreement with the Church which they doubt could have happened 20 or 30 years ago. These instances range from the Government's support for a General Assembly debate of the issue of Communist China's admission to the United Nations down to a small but lively controversy in County Mayo that stirred up widespread interest. A group of Catholic teachers in a public school challenged the right of the local parish priest to appoint a member of a Catholic teaching order as principal of the school—instead of giving the job to one of them. To the disappointment of their admirers all over the country—including many members of the clergy—the laymen eventually compromised, accepting a rise in pay instead of the principalship. Technically they had given in—but the fact of their rebellion was significant.

The proposal late in 1963 to get Catholics to take a pledge in Irish churches not to patronize immoral films, as Catholics have taken the Legion of Decency oath in churches in the United States, met with such resistance that it was quietly dropped. Producers and writers in the Dublin theatre and Irish television say that Church censorship is not at all as restraining as foreigners assume it to be. Jim Fitzgerald, director of *Stephen D.*, Hugh Leonard's dramatization of James Joyce's strongly anticlerical *Portrait of the Artist as a Young Man*, says that the play encountered not even a murmur of complaint when it was staged in Dublin. "But when we did it in London, the Lord High Chamberlain tried to chop it to pieces," he adds. Dubliners blame the notorious Irish censorship of books on the Government rather than on the clergy.

But if the Catholic Church in Ireland is more tolerant today than in the past, it is still too authoritarian for most Irish intellectuals and writers, whose ranks today are probably more filled with rebellious apostates than they were in James Joyce's day. The intellectuals complain that the modern Irish Church is more lenient with trivial and vulgar books and films than it is with those presenting challenging and non-conforming new ideas. Sean O'Faolain contends that there will be no common ground of discussion between Irish intellectual laymen and clergy as long as the priest continues to follow his traditional course of "applying to all intellectual ideas the test of their effect on the poor and the ignorant".

The Irish apostate, always a familiar figure on the Dublin scene, is seldom an atheist. Despite his violent anticlericalism, he cannot shake off the spirituality of his heritage. The most famous of all Irish apostates, Joyce, went to church every year on Holy Thursday and Good Friday long after he broke away from Catholicism. As he himself wrote, "It is a curious thing, do you know, how your mind is supersaturated with the religion in which you say you disbelieve."

L IKE almost everything in Ireland, the severe strictness of the Catholic clergymen of earlier generations was rooted in historical events of the country's past. During the dark era of the anti-Catholic Penal Laws in the 18th century, young Irishmen had to study for the priesthood on the Continent. In the early 1790s, the British Government became alarmed by the rise of Theobald Wolfe Tone's Irish Protestant revolutionary movement (see Chapter 3) and made hurried bids of appeasement to Irish Catholics in an effort to win their loyalty. One of these conciliatory moves was the establishment of the Catholic theological seminary at Maynooth in 1795.

Perhaps not entirely by accident, the faculty of the new college was staffed by refugees from the French Revolution, pro-monarchist theologians who hated Tone's republican ideas. Most of these theologians had been influenced by Jansenism—the rigid and gloomy doctrine,

denounced as Calvinistic by the Jesuits, that man is a helplessly doomed being who must endure punishing soul-searching and rigorous penance to prove his love of God. Mere faith and constant church-going, the Jansenists held, are not enough to win salvation. They attacked the Jesuits for granting absolution for sins leniently, and without assigning sufficient penance to the sinner.

Thanks to the influence of the French theologians at Maynooth, most of the Irish Catholic hierarchy sided with the British against Tone in the rebellion of 1798, and supported William Pitt's Act of Union. Their forbidding and stern Jansenist theory strongly flavoured Irish Catholicism until it was finally officially discouraged in the middle of the 19th century. The last vestiges of the doctrine have long since disappeared from Irish Catholicism, but the unusual devotion of the Irish people today to physically punishing religious pilgrimages could possibly be traced in part back to the old teaching at Maynooth that love of God must be demonstrated by harder acts than receiving the sacraments and going to daily Mass.

One of the most famous of these pilgrimages is the annual climbing of the 2,510-foot rocky slope of Croagh Patrick, the mountain overlooking Clew Bay in County Mayo where Saint Patrick fasted for 40 days and nights and where, according to legend, snakes and other reptiles fled from him. The pilgrims, usually numbering more than 60,000, make the climb before dawn on the last Sunday of July, many of them in bare feet. They stop during the ascent to pray, and finally attend Mass at a chapel on the summit as the sun rises.

O THER groups of pilgrims travel every day during the summer to Lough Derg, a lonely lake in Donegal where Saint Patrick is said to have seen a vision of Purgatory. A striking round-domed Romanesque basilica dedicated to the Saint rises like a mirage on a small island in the middle of the lake. The pilgrims arrive at noon, having fasted from the previous midnight, and spend the next 48 hours in prayer and meditation on the island. They remain awake for all the first night and the next day, sustained only by a piece of dry bread and a cup of black tea, walking around the basilica without shoes while reciting rosaries and other prayers. On the second night they are allowed to sleep in hospices. When they leave the island on the morning of the third day, they fast again until they reach their homes. An 85-year-old man from Enniskillen, Cathal McKeown, made his 65th annual pilgrimage to Lough Derg in 1963.

A NOTABLE new development in the modern Irish Catholic Church is the lay apostolic movement. The conservative hierarchy of the past openly discouraged laymen from reading theological works and from taking an active role in Church work. Until late in the 19th century, most Catholics in Ireland were either illiterate in English or persons with limited education. It was felt that laymen lacking grounding in ecclesiastical learning might cause themselves only harmful confusion by delving too deeply into Church affairs and doctrine. But today many of the most dedicated crusaders for the Church in Ireland are men and women in lay organizations.

One of the strongest of these apostolic movements is the Legion of Mary, a volunteer force devoted to social work and spiritual rehabilitation that has spread all over the world since it was founded in Dublin in 1921. The Legion's active membership in Ireland is more than 100,000, and it sends teachers and lay missionaries to South America, Africa and Asia. The legionaries give a required number of hours each week to charitable service—trying to mend broken marriages, offering guidance to alcoholics and prostitutes, baby-sitting for working mothers, taking turns sleeping overnight in the homes of lone elderly people. The organization gives no material contributions —no food, clothing or money. "That's left to other agencies," explained Frank Duff, the founder and leader of the Legion, not long ago. "We aim only at lifting people's spirit."

The Legion recently completed a mammoth job of spirit-lifting in a parish on the coast of Kerry that was slowly dying from apathy. Its young people were departing. There had been no births in the parish in five years. Hopelessness had settled like a cloud over the entire district; farmland was falling into neglect and homes were beginning to crumble, but the people made no move to help themselves. The worried parish priest appealed to the Legion.

"We went down there and noticed right away what the people themselves had long since failed to see," Duff says. "It was the most beautiful place on earth—the mountain and seaside scenery took your breath away."

With the financial help of the Irish Tourist Board, the Legion workers spent two years persuading the farmers in the parish to renovate their cottages and convert the area into a holiday resort. Agricultural experts showed the people how to profit from the mild Kerry climate by growing high-priced early vegetables. In the summer of 1963 every tourist home in the whole area was sold out for two months. Emigration has stopped and many young people are returning from abroad. "But more important, everybody is smiling and holding up his head again," Duff says.

NOT long ago an elderly priest was discussing the changed relationship between the modern Irish Catholics and the contemporary Irish Catholic Church. He mentioned with amusement that he had heard a popular story at a recent reunion of his class at Maynooth about a Galway clergyman who noticed a young girl from his parish sprawled on a beach wearing a very brief bikini. The priest sent the girl a note, asking her to wear a one-piece bathing suit. She returned a quick reply: "Which piece do you want me to take off?"

The old priest chuckled and said, "I can't imagine an Irish girl handing an answer like that to a priest 30 years ago. But then, of course, 30 years ago Irish girls didn't wear bikinis, now did they?"

A Rose Rooted
in the Nation's Heart

A flower grows more heartily if every bloom but the topmost is sacrificed. Similarly, the Roman Catholic Church in Ireland, representing three quarters of the island's total population, reveals a surprising vigour in spite of, or perhaps because of, its centuries of travail. The Protestant cathedral and the Catholic cathedral on neighbouring hills in Armagh symbolize the religious conflict over the island. Since the reign of Elizabeth I the struggle has raged, and under the 18th-century penal laws, when members of the Roman Church were denied all political and civil rights, the average Catholic learned to fight for his faith. The fervent and deep intimacy established long ago between the priest and his parishioner still prevails.

THE CATHOLIC ENTHRONEMENT by the apostolic nuncio (*seated, far right*) of Dr. William Conway (*at the foot of the steps*) as primate of all Ireland occurs in Saint Patrick's Cathedral. Armagh has been a holy city since it was Saint Patrick's see.

*A PRIEST shows
a tender regard
for his charges
and a scholarly
sense of the past*

VISITING PARISHIONERS in a near-by village (*left*), the Reverend Thomas A. Egan of Ballintubber, County Mayo, chats with one of the 138 families in his parish, near a castle built in the 17th century.

INSPECTING MASONRY which has recently been unearthed, Father Egan surveys progress on his pet project, the restoration of Ballintubber Abbey (*background*), where Mass has been offered for 750 years.

ANSWERING QUESTIONS raised by pupils in school, Father Egan fulfils one of the duties of all village priests, supervision of public education. Schools in the Irish Republic are allied with the Church.

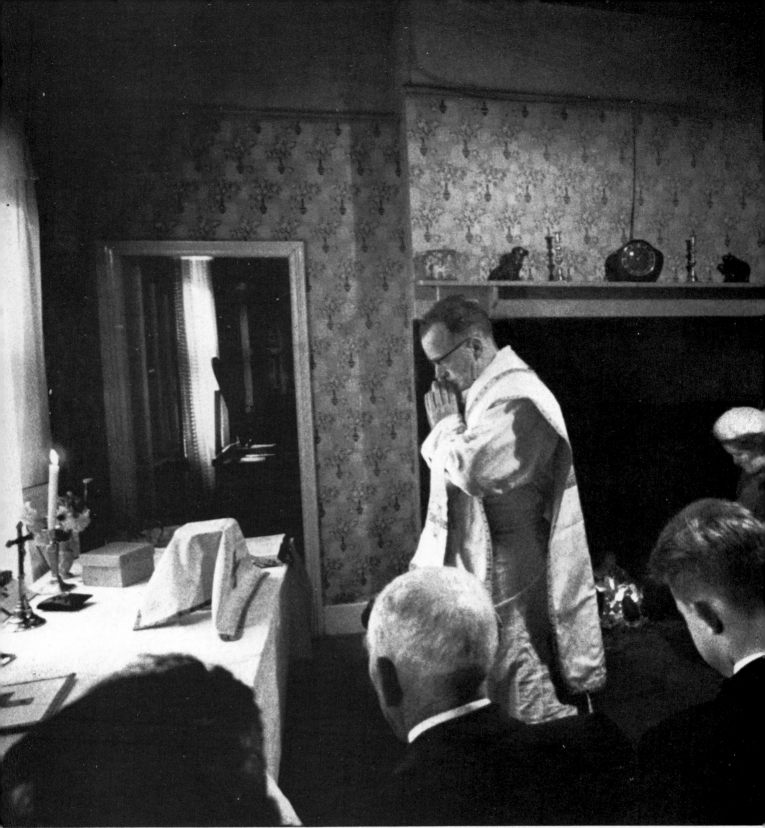

IN A PRIVATE HOME Father Egan celebrates the Mass. During the centuries when Roman Catholics were persecuted in Ireland, the faithful held their services secretly in country cottages. In remembrance of those difficult times the Irish clergy was granted the unique privilege of holding "stations", or the offering of the Mass once a year, in the home of a parishioner.

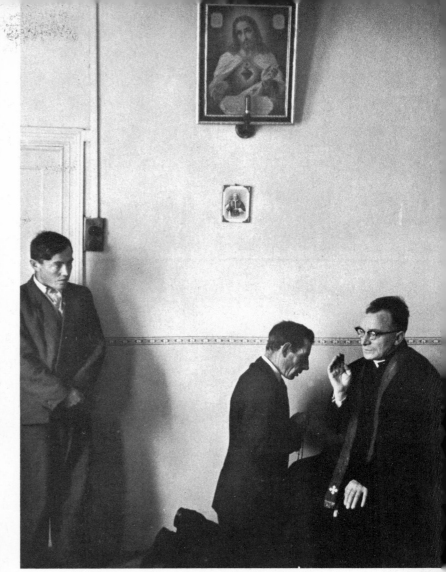

WITH LIFTED HAND, Father Egan grants absolution to Joseph Walsh after hearing his confession in the house of Christy Finnerty, postman of the near-by village of Ballyglass.

THE MASS OVER, Mrs. Jack Hession, in whose home the service was held, serves Father Egan breakfast with the family (*right*). The dining-room was redecorated for the occasion.

AN ECCLESIASTICAL CONFERENCE of Ireland's four archbish-
ops and 24 bishops adjourns in the halls of Saint Patrick's
College, established in 1795 at Maynooth, County Kildare.

A SOLEMN ORDINATION introduces 48 seminarians into the
priesthood at Saint Patrick's College. As the students prostrate
themselves, a bishop prays before ordaining them priests.

THE PRIESTHOOD, a calling
to quiet action and patient service,
begins with a ceremony full of emotion

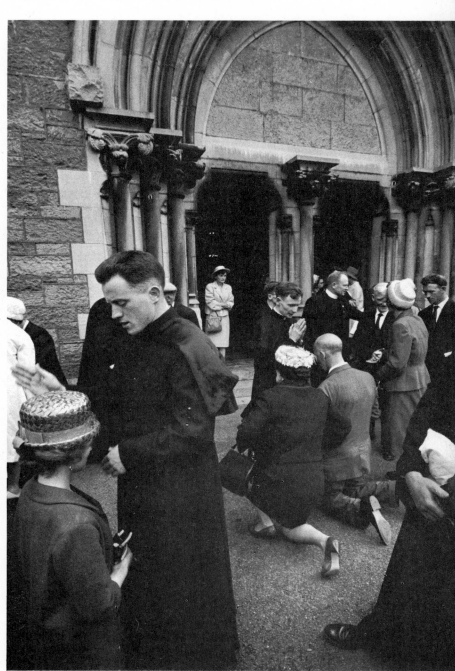

FIRST BLESSINGS given by the new priests are bestowed upon members of their own families. The greatest seminary in Ireland, Saint Patrick's has 500 students engaged in an eight-year course.

6

Masters
of
Language

FOR a small and poor nation, Ireland has produced an astonishing number of the world's great writers. Many of the leading literary figures before 1900 were Irish or of Irish background—Jonathan Swift, Oliver Goldsmith, George Berkeley, William Congreve, Oscar Wilde. Then, in the next 25 years came a spectacular outburst of writing talent from Ireland that gave 20th-century English literature some of its best dramatists, George Bernard Shaw, John Millington Synge and Sean O'Casey; possibly its best poet, William Butler Yeats; and the giant of modern novelists, James Joyce, who has been described as the greatest master of the English language since Milton.

This sparkling array of Irish authors, which also included George Moore, Æ (George Russell), James Stephens, Liam O'Flaherty, Lady Augusta Gregory and Frank O'Connor, emerged suddenly to a position of leadership in the literary world of the new century because they filled a sorely felt need of their time. In the 1890s, literature generally was divided into two extreme schools of writing. One was represented by the murky, romantic lyricism of the French poet Stéphane Mallarmé and the dramas of Oscar Wilde, ornate, artificial and at a remove from the troublesome problems of life. At the opposite pole was the realism of the plays of Henrik Ibsen in Norway and the naturalism of the novels of Émile Zola in France. There was a yearning for writing that would close the wide gap between these two extremes, for the creation of poems, plays and novels dealing with reality and real people, but in rich and colourful language.

The Irish writers were well equipped to satisfy that need. They had poetry; they had humour; they had a hard realism. They reflected the hopes and dreams of common people because their literary movement was linked chronologically and spiritually with the rise of Irish nationalism and the rebellion against Britain. Even the writers themselves were bound up in the nationalist cause. James Joyce's first published piece of writing, composed when he was only nine years old, was *Et Tu, Healy*, a diatribe against a political betrayer of Charles Stewart Parnell, the Home Rule leader. An admirer of Parnell, Joyce's father had it privately printed and proudly handed it out to his friends. William Butler Yeats wrote with deep feeling of the Easter Week uprising of 1916 in his celebrated poem. Two poets prominent in the literary movement, Padraic Pearse and Joseph Mary Plunkett, were executed for their leading parts in that revolt. Sean O'Casey was one of the original organizers of the Irish Citizen Army.

Part of the nationalist movement was the Gaelic League, founded in 1893 to revive Ireland's interest in the Gaelic language and the forgotten native literature of the Middle Ages. This patriotic effort had far-reaching effects. The unearthing of the heroic epics composed by ancient Celtic poets stirred in Yeats, the real father of the modern Irish literary revival, a new appreciation of his native country's heritage, and turned him back to Ireland from the studies of William Blake and theosophy that

he had been pursuing in London. Yeats took another look at the Sligo country, where he had spent much of his youth, and visited the bleak Aran Islands off the western coast of Ireland. He became engrossed in the possibilities for literary material in the dignity, colourful language and rough struggle for existence of the peasants in the west of Ireland. In 1896, Yeats came across Synge studying Racine and other French dramatists in Paris, the accepted course in that period for young men with literary ambitions. He convinced Synge that there was more to be gained from a study of people on the Aran Islands than from reading in French libraries.

"That meeting of two Irishmen in Paris, agreeing that the life of those most remote and barren Arar Islands was the full material for literature, is a parable that marks the final stage of growth of the Irish mind," as the author Sean O'Faolain wrote later. "It was an entirely new thing for men to realize the full and complete dignity of the simplest life of the simplest people. Once they had acknowledged that then they were free to do anything they liked with it in literature—treat it naturalistically, fantastically, romantically, see it in any light they chose. They had conquered their material by accepting it."

Out of this realization and acceptance came such plays as Synge's *Riders to the Sea* and *The Playboy of the Western World*, both first produced at the Abbey Theatre in Dublin. The Abbey, in which Yeats and Lady Augusta Gregory were important figures, brought a fresh breath of real life to theatre audiences long jaded by the fashionable comedies of Wilde, the problem plays of Sir Arthur Wing Pinero, and the flashy melodramas of Dion Boucicault, an Irishman who had enjoyed success in London. The extraordinary freshness, as George Bernard Shaw pointed out approvingly, was

---

IRISH AUTHORS' NAMES

Below is a guide to the pronunciation of the names of some of the more prominent Irish authors who are mentioned in this chapter.

Brendan Behan: Brendan "Bee'-an".

Sean O'Casey: "Shawn" O'-Casey.

Sean O'Faolain: "Shawn O'-Fwaylawn".

Padraic Pearse: "Paw-drick Pierce".

John Millington Synge: John Millington "Sing".

William Butler Yeats: William Butler "Yates".

---

government edifices in the world, but its authority is limited to local matters. All major decisions concerning foreign policy, defence, tariffs and income taxes are made in the Parliament at Westminster. Stormont can impose taxes only on motor vehicles, entertainment and deaths. "Technically the Westminster Parliament is free to legislate for Northern Ireland as if there were no local parliament," the Government information service at Stormont says. However, in practice Stormont's authority within its own field is never challenged, and it is able to legislate on matters of education, social welfare, labour and trade. Income taxes collected by the British Government are turned over to the Government of Northern Ireland, which budgets and spends the money in accordance with its own needs.

As evidence of their difference from the Green Irish, the Orange people point out that Ulster is the only part of Ireland that has been industrialized for the past century. They deny, as the Southern Irish claim, that they were given this economic opportunity by the British because of their Protestantism. It is a matter of racial character, they say, rather than religious discrimination.

THE Ulster Protestants have little of the ancient Irish Celtic ancestry. Their forefathers were the Scottish Presbyterian and English Anglican colonists brought to the Ulster Plantation settlement after the flight of the O'Neill and O'Donnell earls into exile in 1607. They also have a sprinkling of French Protestant ancestry from Huguenot weavers who came from the Continent and started Belfast's textile industry in the 17th century. This background, Ulstermen insist, gave them a natural inclination for mechanical work and for the organization of factory routine. They believe that these talents are not shared by the undisciplined and impractical Celts.

There is no doubt that the Northern Irish Protestants are a different breed from their Catholic neighbours of older native stock. They are more serious and stolid. Their capital city of Belfast, which quickly grew from a small town to a crowded manufacturing centre in the 19th century, has a stern Victorian look unlike that of any of the older cities in the South. All of the north-east corner of Ireland—only 13 miles across the water at one point from Scotland—has a heavy Scottish flavour, and its people speak with a Scottish brogue, using words like "aye", "wee" and "bairn".

NORTHERN Ireland, as the Government of the United Kingdom calls the six Irish counties, and Ulster, as the British territory north of the border is familiarly known, are both misnomers. The area does not include the most northern part of Ireland, Donegal, and it does not cover all the old province of Ulster. Donegal, Cavan and Monaghan are the three old Ulster counties that Carson's Unionists never tried to claim. The Unionists agreed that these three counties on the western and southern edges of the original province of Ulster would be better left outside. Their solidly Catholic and Nationalist populations would have endangered the majority control that the Orange Unionist party hoped to wield —and has wielded—in the provincial Government of Northern Ireland established in 1921.

A contentious issue often raised by Republicans of the South against the partition is the claim that two other Ulster counties, Fermanagh and Tyrone, are also too Catholic and Nationalist to belong to the British. Other predominantly Catholic areas within the partitioned province are the southern parts of Armagh and Down counties and a large section of the county of Derry (renamed Londonderry by the British) that includes the city of Derry. Although the Protestants outnumber the Catholics by 2 to 1 in the six counties' total population of about 1.4 million, most of this Orange two-thirds majority is closely concentrated around Belfast. Yet the Protestant Unionists manage to control local government in all six counties, and they occupy 34 of the 52 seats in the provincial Parliament's House of

Commons and 20 of the 26 seats in its Senate. All 12 of the Northern Ireland members of the United Kingdom's House of Commons at Westminster are Unionists.

The Unionists retain political control in Catholic Nationalist counties by open and unabashed gerrymandering, the arranging of constituencies so that a minority party can elect more officeholders than the opposing majority. A study of gerrymandering in Ulster shows, for example, that in the 1954-5 city council election, the city of Derry, with 31,620 Nationalist and 18,479 Unionist voters, was divided into three wards. Most of the Nationalists were crammed into one ward that could elect only eight of the city's 20 councillors. In the other two wards, which had 12 council seats between them, much smaller contingents of Unionist voters won by adequately safe margins.

Such shenanigans aside, the weakness and disorganization of their opposition have helped the Unionists to maintain control. The Nationalists do not even bother to put up candidates in more than half the traditionally Unionist constituencies.

ANTAGONISM between the two groups has fostered strife and ill-will since partition. One of the most appalling clashes between Orange and Catholic Nationalist Irish—a three-day riot in Belfast in July 1920, in which 18 people were killed and 200 injured—started as a demonstration in the shipyards against Sinn Fein. Belfast at the time was in the throes of one of its periodic industrial slumps; shipbuilding had slowed down and work was scarce. Many Nationalist and British Socialist leaders, among them the late Ramsay MacDonald, have accused Ulster Unionists of deliberately inciting anti-Catholic violence in the times of strain during unemployment to divert resentment from management and Government. "Whenever there is an attempt to root out [sweatshops] in Belfast, the Orange big drum is beaten," MacDonald once said in a House of Commons speech. "Whilst the poor

working classes imagine that this is religious trouble, the people who pay the piper know perfectly well that it is an economic trouble...."

Religious discrimination has had a substantial effect on hiring practices as well. In 1933 Sir Basil Brooke, later Lord Brookeborough, for long the Unionist Prime Minister of Northern Ireland, made a public appeal in a July 12 speech to Orange employers, asking them to hire "good Protestant lads and lassies". For many years Catholic workers had difficulty obtaining jobs in Belfast's two biggest industrial plants, the Harland & Wolff shipyards and the affiliated Short Brothers & Harland aircraft factory. Although religious discrimination has been disappearing in recent years, the unemployment rate remains higher among Catholic workers than among Protestant.

UNEMPLOYMENT has continued to plague Belfast in recent years because shipbuilding and linen-weaving, the city's main sources of jobs, have both been in a steady decline. The shipyards that hired 18,000 workers in 1960—more than 10 per cent of all industrial employees in Ulster that year—provided only 12,500 jobs in 1964. Northern Ireland's 1963 unemployment rate was 8 per cent, compared to 2.5 per cent in the rest of the United Kingdom. Meanwhile the population, unlike that of emigration-troubled Republican Ireland, is showing a constant increase.

To fight unemployment and to overcome its dependence on shipbuilding and the linen trade, Northern Ireland is campaigning to attract new and more diversified industries. The six counties offer a skilled labour force that its neighbour to the south cannot match, Government industrial grants covering a third of plant-building costs and well-developed ports at Belfast, Derry and Larne. The drive is showing results. "If we can create 6,000 new jobs a year, we'll be all right," a Government economist at Stormont says. "And thus far we have got 8,000 such jobs in 1961 and 6,000 more in 1962."

Among the new industrial plants in Ulster are a number bearing impressive British and chance. The wandering tinker families that follow fairs all over the country also mingle on the fringes. These Irish gipsies, or travelling people as they call themselves, trade horses and donkeys while their women, wrapped in bright plaid shawls and often carrying small babies in their arms, beg on street corners and at kitchen doors. The Irish Government has made recent efforts to keep tinkers from camping in their covered wagons on country roads by allocating space for them in low-rent council-house developments. But after a week or two of this indoor living, which they regard as unhealthy, the tinkers vanish.

ON Sunday afternoons in summer and early autumn, Paddy enjoys his favourite relaxation—he is off with a neighbour who has a car to a hurling or football match. The Irish farmer is a fanatical sports lover. In every country pub, the county's hurling and football teams and coaches are endlessly dissected and criticized, and important games of five or 10 years ago are replayed in detail over rounds of stout and beer. After the provincial elimination games, the national championship matches are held in September at Croke Park in Dublin, cheered by crowds of 80,000 and more. Great numbers of the spectators are farmers in rakish tweed caps, puffing excitedly on brier pipes with metal lids on the bowls for protection from the rain.

The county hurling and football teams are strictly amateur organizations. Hurling, a sort of field hockey played with a thick, curved stick of ash and a small ball, requires a deft skill and fine timing. It is a very fast game, fascinating to watch. Parish teams played it in Ireland more than 200 years ago, with hundreds of men and boys on each side knocking the ball across the countryside. Under modern rules, the game is confined to a field somewhat larger than the soccer field layout. The squads have been restricted to 15 men each. The game the Irish call Gaelic football, which has become more popular than hurling, is a combination of rugby and soccer with charging and long kicking, but no tackling.

Because they are such Irish games, hurling and Gaelic football were suppressed in past centuries by the British authorities. They regarded the popular enthusiasm for the sports as a dangerous display of nationalism. The Gaelic Athletic Association, organized in 1884 to revive the games, established a retaliatory rule, still in effect today, forbidding any member of its football and hurling teams to play such British sports as cricket, soccer or rugby. Another defiantly patriotic rule of the Association, now relaxed, forbade its members from even watching non-Irish sports.

When he was younger Paddy was devoted, like a lot of other farmers, to road bowling, a peculiarly Irish game that has been hampered in recent years by the increase in motor traffic. The bowlers, backed by lively betting, roll small iron balls along country roads, striving for distance rather than marksmanship. They try to cover a certain number of miles in the fewest number of throws.

The Irish countrymen, especially the younger, unmarried men, are avid followers of greyhound racing. Almost every large town has a greyhound track. In the counties of Dublin, Meath, Cork and Tipperary, and at the National Open Cup meeting in Kildare, dogs are raced, as they were centuries ago, across open fields. All the Irish, country folk and town people alike, flock to horse races run on great sweeping courses of turf like those seen in old sporting prints.

ON the day of the Irish Sweepstakes Derby, the bar under the grandstand at the Curragh in Kildare, which claims to be the longest in the world—it stretches more than 100 yards—is thronged four deep with men reaching over other men's shoulders for drinks and talking about the last or the next race. On every other corner in every city and large town, there is an office of a "turf accountant", the Irish bookmaker's dignified name for his profession. The gala period of the Dublin year, with hotels overflowing and parties every night, is the week of the Royal Dublin Society's August Horse

Show and world jumping competition, one of the most colourful sports spectacles in the world.

While more frequent today, such days of leisure are rare for the Irish farmer. To prosper, even to survive, he must give his time to his land. Paddy Dolan is what Irish agricultural officials call a broad-minded farmer; he attends farm-association meetings and keeps in touch with the latest theories on land improvement and livestock breeding. He has been observing with interest the recent success of sugar-beet growing in Ireland. The state-owned Irish Sugar Company buys beet crops from farmers on a contract basis and operates four refineries which export sugar. Paddy would be inclined to try beet growing if he had a few more acres.

Since a fine hay crop cannot be counted on every year, he is also interested in building a silo to store a good harvest for the winter feeding of his stock. The Government would pay part of the costs if he constructed a silo, but Paddy would have to build it before his grant could be approved, and that, of course, would require capital. He plans to accumulate the money by increasing the milk yield from his stock with the guidance of the Government's experts, but he realizes that it will take time and luck to save the money.

"So I go along, making enough to keep me going from day to day, and hoping to put aside capital for the improvements and the extra acreage that my farm needs," Paddy says. "However, I read in a newspaper that Ireland has a lower suicide rate than other European countries and that Irish farmers have less heart disease than their brothers in Boston." But he adds, "I don't have a brother in Boston, so perhaps that doesn't apply to me."

A COUPLE of rungs above Paddy Dolan on the economic ladder are the Irish farmers whose more prosperous status can be readily spotted from the road by the appearance of their houses, substantial two-storey buildings of brick or stucco rather than small cottages, and their large barns, which today are often roofed with new corrugated iron.

Higher yet, at the top of the scale, are the big and well-kept farms with the handsome Georgian homes built in the 18th century by wealthy Anglo-Irish Protestant landowners. Their large, high-ceilinged rooms contain original, exquisite furniture and bookshelves filled with beautifully bound 300-year-old volumes of Molière and Cervantes. Many of these manors are still occupied by descendants of the same families that built them. They are the titled gentry who show off their hunters at the Dublin Horse Show. "The difference between *them* and us," a small farmer says, "is that when they go out of their house, nobody knows where they're going. If we're not home, we're at Pat Mulligan's or Seamus Casey's, but *they* are likely to be in London or somewhere on the Riviera."

A PROSPEROUS farmer with a choice collection of antiques in his home is an old friend of Paddy Dolan named Joseph Purcell, a well-known cattle and horse auctioneer who operates a 228-acre farm with 500 head of livestock in Birr, County Offaly. Joe Purcell feels that the smaller Irish farmer is being left in the shadows by the Government's emphasis on industrialization. "This country is an agricultural one, but all the Government talks about is industry," Purcell says. "We could greatly improve our general economic picture if we took some steps towards improving Ireland's farm marketing system and supplying fellows like Paddy Dolan with a little more financial help. We can produce beef here cheaper than anybody in Europe. Why not take advantage of that opportunity?"

Government economists in Dublin are not in agreement with the belief that their industrialization plan overlooks the farmer. On the contrary, they say, more industrial jobs will slow the emigration of farm boys from Ireland, build a larger market for Irish farm produce and enable marginal farmers to sell their land and take factory work, thus creating larger farms—and larger farms are precisely what Paddy Dolan and his neighbours need.

In a field behind their homes in County Mayo, five boys practise the old Irish sport of hurling, a fast game similar to field hockey.

A Passionate Love for All Sports and Pageants

Enthusiasm for sports is Ireland's national tonic. A consuming interest in the fortunes of his county hurling team enlivens the arduous life of the farmer. The ennui of the office-worker is forgotten as he cheers his favourite Gaelic football team. A love for the country's fine horses burns in the hearts of all Irishmen, from the gentry who ride to hounds to the small punter who wagers a few shillings with the "turf accountant". Horse-trading is a part of many local fairs, and the leading social event in all Ireland is the Dublin Horse Show. From the fine style of the Horse Show as well as from the mayhem of a football match shine forth the gaiety and spirit of what William Butler Yeats called "the indomitable Irishry".

A SHARP COLLISION occurs between Galway (dark jerseys) and Dublin players during 1963 All-Ireland finals.

A HOME PLAYER is carried from the field (*below*) by Dublin fans after their victory over the Galway team.

EXUBERANT SPECTATORS wearing the colours of County Meath (*opposite*) cheer their team during a match.

GAELIC FOOTBALL, *dating from medieval times, attracts partisan crowds*

A YOUNG HORSEWOMAN, Miss Antoinetta O'Regan, hugs her pony while talking to friends in the stables at the Dublin Horse Show. The Show has several events for fledgling riders.

A CROUCHING COMPETITOR takes a handsome horse over a water-jump (*below*) as a top-hatted steward looks on. Participants from half a dozen nations compete regularly at the Show.

DUBLIN'S HORSE SHOW, *held every summer, draws riders and horse-lovers from all over Europe*

AN ELEGANT ARISTOCRAT, Althea Urquhart, riding side-saddle in traditional top-hat and hunting dress, displays her hunter, Edmund Spenser, during an event on the Show's Ladies' Day.

NATIONAL JUMPING TEAMS heralded by a pipe band (*left*) parade past the flower-bordered stands before competing for the Aga Khan Trophy. The Irish won the trophy in 1963.

PUCK FAIR, *a mixture*
of carnival and hard-headed commerce,
is held each August in Killorglin

AN HONOURED GOAT, ready to preside as "King" of Puck Fair, is adorned by the Queen, wearing her crown, and helpers before it is hoisted high on a platform in the town square.

EXPERIENCED HORSE-TRADERS turn a critical eye on each other's offerings (*opposite*) during the second day of Puck Fair. The fair offers both carnival rides and wide-open pubs.

HERDS OF CATTLE, unnoticed by men gathered in a pub door, rumble through the streets of Killorglin (*right*) on their way to the livestock market which takes up the fair's third day.

hurl an iron ball to a distant finishing-post

A LEAPING BOWLER, Donal Lehane, aims his iron ball towards a friend (*background*) who has calculated the route round a corner. Strong bowlers make throws of 200 yards and more.

A GRIMLY INTENT CROWD watches Johnny Creedon limber up to throw his 28-ounce cast-iron bowl in a recent match (*left*). Road bowling is very popular in the environs of Cork.

A COUNTRY-LIFE TABLEAU is formed by Montague Kavanaugh, his wife and their children as they ride a donkey cart on the grounds of Dolland, the Kavanaugh home near Dublin.

EAGER HOUNDS, urged on by red-coated riders (*right*), ford the River Claddy in a scene reminiscent of the 18th century as the Meath Hunt pursues a fox across the fertile countryside.

A PEACEFUL BOAT RIDE on an inlet which borders part of their magnificent 18th-century country estate, Westport House, is enjoyed by the young Earl and Countess of Altamount.

RURAL PLEASURES both placid and vigorous fill the lives of the Irish gentry

9

The Advancing Middle Class

"THE country is steadily advancing," wrote the British author William Makepeace Thackeray in 1842, "not nearly so wretched now as it was a score of years since; and let us hope that the *middle class*, which this increase of prosperity must generate (and of which our laws have hitherto forbidden the existence in Ireland, making there a population of Protestant aristocracy and Catholic peasantry), will exercise the greatest and most beneficial influence over the country. Too independent to be bullied by priest and squire—having their interest in quiet, and alike indisposed to servility or to rebellion; may not as much be hoped from the gradual formation of such a class as from any legislative meddling?"

Thackeray's 1842 comment on Ireland's need for a substantial middle class could have been written by another visiting observer in 1942 and yet once more in 1952. Over the past century the kind of Irish people capable of forming a stabilizing layer of population between the poor, small farmer and the wealthy, landed gentry were steadily forced to emigrate from the country for lack of economic opportunity. As recently as 20 years ago the Republic of Ireland was importing everything it needed except food. There was still so little industry in

131

the Republic in 1952 that a guide-book published by the Government in that year offered the country's lack of factory smoke as a lure to tourists.

Under the economics-minded leadership of the Prime Minister, Sean Lemass, who would squirm if he heard Ireland praised for being smokeless, the long hoped-for sizeable middle class is at last becoming a reality. More than 160 new industrial plants have gone up since 1955 and many others are under construction. The rate of emigration has dropped off. The leisurely, tweedy Anglo-Irish aristocrats, described by the writer Brendan Behan as "Protestants who own horses", are being outnumbered at cocktail time in Dublin's Shelbourne and Royal Hibernian hotels by brisk, young, native-born business executives who did not go to Trinity, Oxford or Cambridge. One of them complained a while ago about a pictorial study of modern Ireland in an American travel magazine.

"According to that magazine, all Irish people live either in thatched cottages or in castles," he said. "The only Irish people I know in Ireland aren't that poor or that rich—they live in plain, ordinary brick or stucco houses with curtains or Venetian blinds on the windows, electric stoves in the kitchen, flower boxes on the front porch and washing hanging out to dry on the line in the back yard, just like the houses I've seen in Queens on the way from Idlewild airport to New York City."

SUCH a house in a development of many exactly similar and closely adjoining houses —small and brick, with six rooms, a tiny front lawn and a little back garden—is located in north-west Dublin near Phoenix Park. It is the home of a 42-year-old man we shall call Liam Sheehan, his wife Maureen, and their six lively young children. The Sheehans may be described as fairly typical members of the expanding middle class; Liam's job as personnel supervisor in an industrial plant did not exist in Dublin a few years ago. If it did not exist today, Liam would probably be living and working in Britain or in the U.S.A. instead of in Ireland.

Irish to the core, and deeply attached to their ageing parents, who live near by, Liam and Maureen are glad to be living in Dublin. But there is a big drawback in working as an industrial employee in a country, like Ireland, over-supplied with manpower for too few jobs and over-eager to please new management's every whim. To qualify for his supervisory position, Liam had to take university-level courses in business administration at night, under considerable hardship and financial sacrifice. Yet he is so replaceable that he is paid no more than £1,375 a year—about half what his younger brother earns as an electrician in New York.

IRISH Government economists contend that the Sheehans with their £1,375 can live as well in Ireland as a family lives in America on $10,000. The economists point out that the best sirloin steak is 4s. 6d. a pound in Dublin, that the best seats in the Abbey or Gate theatres are 10s. 6d., that a membership in the best golf club costs £20 a year and that a caddie's fee for 18 holes is 7s. These figures make no impression on Liam Sheehan.

"I'm sure a bachelor could live very well on what I earn," he says. "I know a bachelor who has a nice room with breakfast and supper, plus dinner on Sundays, for five guineas a week. But I assure you that when you're supporting a wife and six children on a salary like mine, you eat precious little sirloin steak, you never go to the theatre and you don't play golf."

The Sheehans' financial lot is somewhat eased by the fact that Ireland's standard of living is simpler and far less costly than those of more prosperous countries. The Irish feel no obligation to provide many of the luxuries that an industrial employee in California or Pennsylvania gives to his family. The two teenage Sheehan daughters, Kathy and Eileen, do not dawdle on the telephone, for instance, because they do not have one. Telephones are still unusual in Irish homes; the telephone directory for the entire Republic of Ireland—including

Dublin, which takes up half the book—is smaller than that of Brooklyn. Motor-cars are almost as scarce; there are only 74 family cars for every thousand people in the population. Many workers in Dublin ride to their jobs on bicycles.

Ireland had no television station until 1961, when the Republican Government owned and operated Telefís Eireann opened its modern studios in the Donnybrook section of Dublin. (The Ulster Government has its own television station, broadcasting from Belfast.) Irish television is supported by licence fees paid by set holders and its programmes are not usually sponsored, but commercials are shown during programme breaks.

Liam Sheehan gave in recently under pressure from his children and bought a television set, paying like most Irish TV owners an extra £20 or so for a special aerial to pick up the British Broadcasting Corporation programmes from Britain in addition to Telefís Eireann shows. As Liam feared, television has filled his living-room at all hours of the evening with neighbours of all ages. Irish television goes on the air around five o'clock in the afternoon on weekdays (a few hours earlier with sports events at week-ends) and signs off at 11 o'clock at night. Like the B.B.C., it shows many runs of American entertainment shows and westerns—"The Jack Benny Programme", "The Phil Silvers Show", "The Flintstones", "Leave it to Beaver", "Gunsmoke", "Bat Masterson"—interspersed with live native drama, religious programmes ("Benediction of the Blessed Sacrament" every Sunday at six), symphony concerts, and variety programmes featuring the pop groups such as the Royals, the Rebels and the Clipper Carltons, that are the rage of Ireland's crowded dance-halls.

POP music also blasts from the Irish radio, making Maureen Sheehan grumble about the suffering that the United States is inflicting on the rest of the world. She has laid down a rule that Kathy and Eileen, now 15 and 14, must not set foot in a dance-hall until they are at least 18. Both girls are adept twisters, having picked up the steps from friends. (A favourite Irish twisting tune is called "Twisting in the Gloaming".)

Liam, like many parents elsewhere, is praying that television will not distract his youngsters from the habit of reading. After Kathy and Eileen come Mary, 11, John, 9, and Michael, 7, and then Peggy, 18 months. "They're all bookworms, except Peggy, of course, and I want to keep them that way," Liam says. Maureen and Liam, like many of the Irish, are book addicts themselves. Both of them have read their favourite novel, Tolstoy's immense *War and Peace*, from cover to cover four times. They complain because their local public library in Dublin allows only three books a week to each adult member.

THE television set is the Sheehans' only outstanding luxury. Their motor-car, a small, four-cylinder Fiat that Liam was able to buy second-hand for £300 with a £200 allowance on his previous car, is for him a real necessity. Unlike many urban husbands who are away at their jobs all day, Liam, like most Irishmen, takes enough time off from his job at noon to eat his big meat-and-potatoes meal of the day at home. This means, of course, that he drives back and forth to his office twice a day.

The old-fashioned custom of eating dinner at noon and a light supper in the evening may account for the slimness of both men and women in Ireland; a foreign visitor realizes after a few days that he has seen few fat people. Then, too, food is not the passion in Ireland that it is in countries like France and Italy. Cooking is a necessary chore rather than an artistic ceremony, and the Irishman will usually eat anything put in front of him without bothering overmuch about its flavour or seasoning.

Maureen Sheehan feeds her family with an economy that would impress many housewives. She spends around £10 a week for meat, groceries and milk. As little as this seems for a table of six children and two grown-ups, it leaves the Sheehans with only about £15 to cover all their other weekly living expenses because Liam's annual income of £1,375 amounts to approximately £26 5s. a week.

THE Sheehans are able to make ends meet (albeit with considerable financial strain) because the Government of the Republic (which has never recognized the Soviet Union) is closer to socialism than it admits. (Together with Telifis Eireann and Radio Eireann, the Government owns Irish Airlines, the country's single electric power utility company, and the Irish peat-fuel and sugar-beet industries and railways. A third of private industrial concerns are heavily subsidized by the Government.) In the areas of education, housing, medical service and social security, an Irish family with six children in the Sheehans' income bracket gets a big parental helping hand from the state.

The standing charges on the Sheehans' three-bedroom home, for example, come to only a little more than £73 a year. The land was sold to Liam a few years ago by the Dublin city council on a 99-year mortgage which costs him only about £8 a year, and the house was built for £570, payable over a 35-year period at £65 a year.

The heavy local education rate which plagues householders in many Western countries are unknown in Ireland; the national Government pays the entire bill for state education. The rate on Liam's house and property, another of the Sheehans' larger expense items, amounts to £50 a year. All secondary schools in the country, both academic and vocational, are private institutions, usually religious, but the Government pays a grant for each pupil and 75 per cent of the teachers' salaries. Consequently, the tuition fee for Kathy and Eileen Sheehan in a near-by private high school, with Dominican nuns as teachers, comes to only £15 a year each.

Because of deductions for his six children, Liam pays no income tax. In addition the Government pays the Sheehans a monthly family allowance for children under 16—10s. for the first child, 15s. 6d. for the second one and 26s. 6d. for each subsequent child. In the case of the Sheehans, with six eligible youngsters, this adds up to £6 11s. 6d. a month. All Irish families, regardless of how wealthy they may be, are paid such an allowance. Well-to-do parents save it for their children's university education, but Maureen uses hers for her family's clothing.

IRELAND does not have a National Health Service like Britain, but a government health insurance plan, with an annual premium of £17, covers the Sheehans' doctor's and hospital bills. A social security payment of £68 a year will entitle Liam to retire on half-pay when he reaches 65.

A conservative-minded American critic of the welfare state, wondering how a small Government like Ireland's can indulge in such social spending without going broke, might find part of the answer in the Republic's defence costs. The annual cost of the green-uniformed Irish Army of 8,000 men is a fifth of what New York City pays for refuse collection each year. The cost of government is generally infinitesimal in Dublin compared to what it is in Washington. Rather than inhabit an impressive establishment, the Irish chief executive, the Prime Minister, Sean Lemass, lives in a seven-room suburban bungalow. There are few big public buildings. Government offices are scattered around the capital city in old Georgian houses, where they share office space and letter boxes with physicians, lawyers and insurance brokers.

As Thackeray predicted, most members of the rising Irish middle class are independent but quiet people, not given to either servility or rebellion. The Sheehans' main interests are their family and their home. Ireland's suburbia has little civic or community activity beyond the social life of the parish church, with its amateur theatricals, dances and badminton and bowling leagues, or sometimes a Boy Scout troop.

"My sister lives in Park Forest, Illinois, near Chicago, and she says the husbands and wives there are going to various organization meetings every night of the week," Maureen Sheehan says. "It's not that way in Ireland at all. We're always at home with our kids, perhaps too much so I think at times. Liam and I have never had a holiday alone together in the 16 years of our married life. When we do get away in the summer, it's an outdoor camping trip to Kerry or Donegal and all the children are with us. Our only vice is cigarettes—two packets a day between us, much more than we can afford, but then we have to do something!"

Liam has never been actively involved in politics, somewhat to the disappointment of his father, a rabid Sinn Feiner who served in action with the I.R.A. during the rebellion and the subsequent civil war. Some years ago the elder Sheehan tried to interest his son in the modern underground "new I.R.A.", dedicated to terrorism in Ulster to break down the partition, but Liam would have none of it.

LIKE most Irishmen of his generation, born after The Troubles and never having heard a shot fired in patriotic anger, Liam regrets the partition because he feels Ireland urgently needs economic union with industrialized Ulster, but he is against blowing up bridges and customs stations at the border. Furthermore, also like most Irishmen his age, he holds no hard grudge against the British. His industrial plant is British-financed and he works under British bosses, getting along fine with them. "Much better fellows than some Irish bosses I've had," he says. Although he listens respectfully to his father's stories about Michael Collins and Terence MacSwiney and the raids of the Black and Tans, that kind of passionate hatred for the British is in fact something which he does not fully understand.

Modern Irish politics, reflecting the sober thinking of Liam Sheehan's industrial middle class, is much tamer than it used to be. There is no longer a strongly anti-British faction to enliven the polemics in the Dail, the national parliamentary arena, as there was only a few years ago. Under the leadership of Eamon de Valera, the dominant Fianna Fail party carried on the old anti-treaty and anti-partition Republican crusade of the civil war. It was this group —with widespread popular support—that kept Ireland neutral in World War II, despite the fact that the Dublin Government then belonged to the British Commonwealth as a free state, like Canada and Australia. The opposition party, Fine Gael, represented the pro-treaty, and somewhat more pro-British, Free Staters of the civil war. Its present leader, James M. Dillon, was the only prominent Irish politician to make a stand against de Valera's neutrality during the war.

BUT now there is little, if any, ideological difference between the two parties, even though they squabble furiously over domestic policies. When de Valera retired from the Fianna Fail leadership in 1959, moving upstairs to the non-political Presidency, he carried with him the last vestiges of the uncompromisingly anti-British spirit of the revolution. His successor, Sean Lemass, was, of course, himself a former I.R.A. fighter who served a year in a Free State jail after the civil war. Without such a record he would never have gained the job of party leader. But Sean Lemass realizes more than Eamon de Valera ever did that Ireland's economy depends on a friendly working relationship with Britain, its best customer as well as its biggest creditor. However much they may disagree on other matters, the two Irish political parties are joined as one in support of the policy of friendship with the kingdom on the opposite shore of the Irish Sea. The bond which William Pitt failed to tie by his Act of Union at the beginning of the 19th century seems now to be knotted by the realities of 20th-century economics, which nobody respects more than the hard-working people of Ireland's new middle class.

Fresh Confidence Breeding New Energy

A new mood of confidence is abroad in Ireland as the country rouses itself from a long period of inertia. Factories are going up, creating new jobs and cutting emigration. Ireland's youth is not only remaining at home, but is also determined to prepare itself, through education, for a role in making the country a modern nation. Heirs to a humanist tradition which was flowering even before the Middle Ages, the Irish have begun to concentrate on such 20th-century preoccupations as electronics and economics. In factories and classrooms a new energy reflects Ireland's turn from self-pity to self-help.

SERIOUS YOUNG STUDENTS in a County Donegal school work through a Gaelic recitation after putting some Gaelic phrases on the blackboard. Gaelic is taught in all state schools.

A row of cheerful girls perches on the whitewashed roadside wall before a handsome new school in Newmarket-on-Fergus, County Clare.

THE AWE-INSPIRING EXAMINATION HALL of Trinity College, Dublin, rises above a few students bending over their exams. Known as the Theatre, the hall was built between 1779 and 1791.

The most renowned of Ireland's colleges, Trinity dates back to 1591 when it was founded by Queen Elizabeth I. It has for long rivalled Oxford and Cambridge in excellence of scholarship.

Ireland has a strong educational tradition, and the Government is expending increasing amounts to support and improve the school system.

A FAMILY in Dublin,
the Boylans live
in modest comfort as the
children energetically
pursue their educations

A COFFEE-BREAK with her friends enlivens registration day (*right*) at University College, Dublin, for Anna Boylan
(*centre*), the Boylans' eldest daughter.
She is working for a degree in economics.

A NEAT BEDROOM-STUDY surrounds
21-year-old Hugo Boylan (*opposite*), a
serious student of chemical engineering
at University College. All four Boylan
children attend good schools or colleges.

AFTER-DINNER DISCUSSION brings
together the whole Boylan family (*below*)
in their comfortable drawing-room. The
father, Henry Boylan (*far left*), is a civil
servant and a student of Gaelic literature.

BEWIGGED BARRISTERS greet clients in the columned rotunda at Dublin's Four Courts (*above*), a magnificent Georgian structure that now houses Ireland's High Court of Justice.

CHEERFULLY BLAZING LIGHTS are reflected in the walls and mirrors of Jammet's restaurant in Dublin (*below*). Jammet's is famous for its steaks and the liveliness of its law clientele.

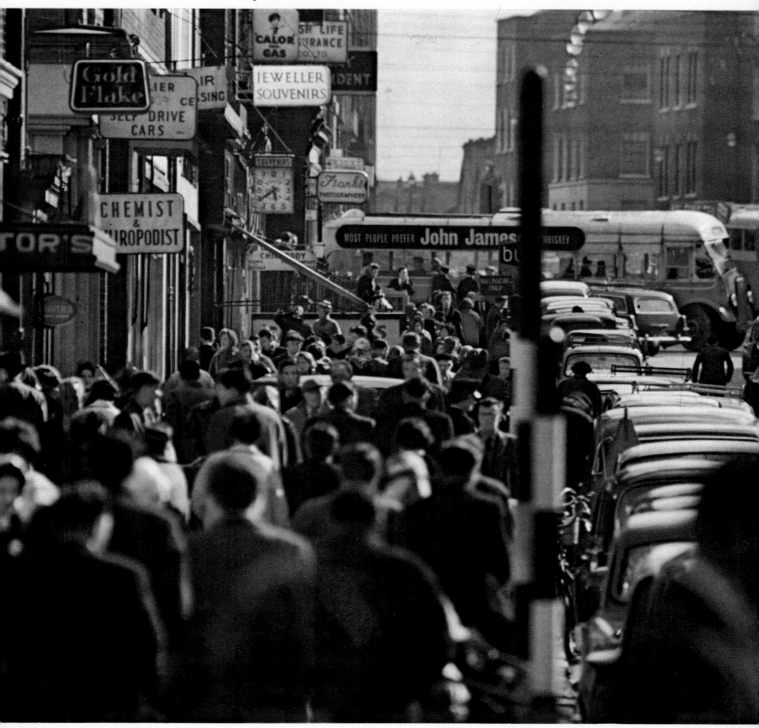

A JAMMED THOROUGHFARE, O'Connell Street, Limerick, is crowded at rush-hour by cars, buses and massed pedestrians. Its 50,000 inhabitants make Limerick Ireland's fourth largest city. With good dock facilities on the River Shannon, Limerick imports many of the materials needed by the plants which surround Shannon Airport and ships much of the plants' produce.

A REFURBISHED FACTORY makes the famous Waterford crystal as men shape the molten glass (*left*). Long idle, the Waterford factory reopened in 1952 with 45 workers. It now employs more than 800.

AN UP-TO-DATE MACHINE covered with spindles of bright yarn (*right*) knits sweaters for export at a plant near Shannon Airport. Irish knitwear and tweeds find ready markets in Europe and America.

MODERNITY comes
as new plants and
apartment houses rise
and old industries
are revitalized

SMART FLATS, housing workers
from factories near Shannon Airport (*left*), overlook a customs shed
on the edge of the duty-free area.
Freedom from customs duty has
helped build Shannon's industry.

CROSSING THE HARBOUR, a fishing-boat pulls away from a stone pier in Waterford on a clear spring morning. In the fishing village of Ballyhack, County Wexford, stands a castle which was sacked by the forces of Oliver Cromwell in 1649.

10

Ourselves No Longer Alone

THE big change of the 1960s in Ireland, shaping a new course for the future, is the country's abandonment of its stubborn nationalism of the last half-century. Seven hundred years of persecution under British rule, climaxed by the bitter memory of the famine, drew the already clannish Irish closer together in hurt resentment long before they won political independence in 1921. When that freedom finally came, it touched off an eruption of suppressed national pride that swelled Ireland with a smug delusion of self-sufficiency.

When the acutely nationalist revolutionary leader Eamon de Valera took over the Government in 1932, he launched a 25-year effort to isolate the country as a sort of idealistic refuge of Gaelic culture, aloof from the fast-changing modern world. De Valera waged an economic war against Britain and threw up high tariff barriers against foreign trade in an attempt to promote home industry—while discouraging foreign investments in Ireland. De Valera's protectionist policies had some success. A number of small industries sprang up to supply basic Irish needs, though many of the new firms were inefficient producers and their products were of low quality. Many economists today feel that the protectionist policies were basically sound, but carried out with little discrimination. The old leader of Sinn Fein (Ourselves Alone) seemed unwilling to face the hard fact that a small island like Ireland, with no oil and only a little iron and coal in its soil—and no emeralds—could never be industrially self-sustaining.

Trying to stop imports, de Valera even went to the extent of asking the Irish people to drink milk and beer instead of tea, their favourite beverage. The drive against tea was not much more futile than de Valera's campaign to make the Irish speak Gaelic, still one of the Government's two official languages—English is the other—and compulsory in the national schools.

THE attempt to revive a native language spoken nowhere in the world except on Ireland's west and south-west coasts and in the highlands of Scotland was, of course, carrying nationalism to impractical extremes. But de Valera persisted in using economic and political pressure to push the change in language. He became so emotionally involved in this crusade that in one public address he declared that the speaking of Gaelic was more important than Ireland's political freedom, an exaggeration that he could not really have meant. The Gaelic-language campaign became a symbol of the whole nationalist movement, and the failure of Gaelic to replace English paralleled the realization by the Irish that nationalism could not cure their country's economic ills.

"There seems to be a lot of associations holding meetings and talking a lot about the Irish language," a reader wrote to the editor of the *Connacht Tribune*. "If there was only half as much meetings about jobs for people, the people might be better off. I don't expect any of these Gaelic League people, or whatever they are, care a thrawneen [straw] for my three sons, but I care for them and I would rather hear them speak English as they worked in a Galway factory or in a Galway shop than know they could talk Irish to themselves as they worked on an English railway station."

During the administration of de Valera, covering all but six of the 27 years between 1932 and 1959, emigration steadily drained away Ireland's young people. A general exodus headed for Britain's defence-plants during World War II, while isolated Ireland remained neutral and unstirred by wartime industry. This colony of emigrants stayed on in England after the war, and jobs similar to theirs attracted other Irishmen in the post-war years. "As a result of the demand for wartime workers, there must be more than a million Irish people in England now," an official in Dublin said recently. The emigrants left behind them a country sorely depressed by lack of industrial employment. In an article about his country, Frank O'Connor wrote in 1949, "There is considerable, and sometimes dreadful, poverty. . . . The standard of life is low. The main food of the poorer classes is bread and tea with potatoes and an occasional egg and sausage. . . . Continuous emigration, the feeling that people are fighting a losing battle, induces a feeling of despondency."

THEN, at the beginning of the 1960s, a breath of fresh air swept through the Republic of Ireland. The austere Eamon de Valera, who for all his indifference to harsh economics did more than any Irishman to make his nation free, retired from political leadership in 1959 and was elected to the non-executive Presidency. His successor as Fianna Fail party leader and Prime Minister, Sean Lemass, is a driving industrial innovator. Moving fast to attract foreign investors, the Lemass Government rid itself of the hard protective shell of ingrown nationalism. Not only did new industry come in; Ireland came out to join the world.

Signs of a spirited break from narrow provincialism were seen everywhere—in New York and in Africa as well as in Ireland itself. The President of the United Nations General Assembly who called Khrushchev to order when he staged his shoe-thumping tantrum against Dag Hammarskjöld was an Irishman, Frederick H. Boland. In contrast to its past reluctance to become involved in foreign disputes, Ireland shouldered military arms for the U.N. in the Congo. Instead of "The Wearing of the

Green" and the sad ballad of Kevin Barry, the I.R.A. youth hanged by the British during The Troubles, Irish schoolchildren now sing a popular patriotic song about the Irish soldiers who were killed in Katanga in 1960.

In fact, observers at the U.N. have noted that Ireland is taking up a role of importance in international affairs out of all proportion to its size and political power. Ireland has stepped on the toes of both East and West. It annoyed the French by becoming the first Western European nation to call for self-determination in Algeria. It infuriated the Communists by bringing up the issue of Communist China's aggression in Tibet and irritated others by urging the U.N. to re-examine the question of whether Peking or Taiwan should represent China.

The Irish themselves explain this increasing prominence in world politics by pointing out that they have a special position of seniority among smaller countries because their Republic was the first of the modern ex-colonial nations.

"Such countries as India, Egypt, Algeria and Nigeria trust us and look to us for guidance because we've been through the problems they're going through now," an Irish Government official observes. "Furthermore, they respect us because we've stayed free and clear of deep involvement with the big powers. That's why they feel safe in sending so many of their young people to Ireland for education and political and technical training. If anybody wonders what Ireland's future role in the world will be, there's the answer. As the leader of an increasingly powerful bloc of uncommitted ex-colonial nations, Ireland will be playing a very important role in the years to come."

SEAN LEMASS agrees, but adds that the prestige of Ireland in the new nations is not entirely due to their similar political backgrounds. "Our Irish missionaries who have worked for generations in those countries are also responsible for the trust they have in us," Lemass says. "Ireland to a lot of those people is a kind man in a Roman collar or a woman in a nun's habit who befriended them years ago."

How long Ireland can remain politically independent of the big powers in the economic pressure of today's world is a matter of lively conjecture in Dublin. One of Lemass's opponents in the Irish Parliament has asserted that the late President Kennedy's wildly acclaimed visit to the homeland of his great-grandparents in 1963 was a prelude to the establishment of an American military base at the strategically located Shannon Airport.

THE Government shrugs off such speculation, which arises partly from Shannon's economic problems. Before the jet age it was a thriving refuelling stop for commercial trans-atlantic airliners. The longe-range jets can now bypass Ireland on their flights from America to Europe. But Shannon is adjusting through the rapid expansion of an already large complex of factories for foreign industrialists within the almost totally tax-free and completely duty-free area of its international airport.

The Shannon offer of manufacturing facilities without taxes or duties is typical of the generous inducements extended by the Lemass Government to foreign-financed industry which will create new jobs in Ireland. The Republic's Government provides non-repayable grants covering up to two thirds of the cost of a new plant and its machinery. Some of these subsidies have come to as much as £215,000.

Such progress is producing the desired effects: Ireland's emigration rate, which reached 56,000 in 1957, came down to an estimated 25,000 in 1963, and may well be less than that in the next few years. The increase in jobs— and the stimulating change in the whole spirit and outlook of the country—is not only cutting emigration. It is also bringing back Irish workers from Britain.

"We can assure a prospective employer that he can get all the skilled labour he needs merely by dropping a help-wanted-in-Ireland advertisement into a British newspaper," Lemass says. "A manufacturer of electronic parts in Cork will find plenty of experienced Corkmen in English electronic plants who will jump at the chance to do the same work at home."

The Dublin Government regards the first phase of its long-range industrial development programme—the drive to make the country self-sufficient in consumer goods—as well under way. Now aiming at building an export trade, it points proudly at 77 new plants built in the Republic by foreign investors in 1960 and 1961 alone, and a jump in industrial exports from £23 million in 1958 to £62 million in 1963, an increase of 168 per cent.

Lemass is now launching an ambitious six-year economic development drive to raise the Republic's gross national product 50 per cent by 1970. "We assume that we'll be in the European Common Market by that time," the Prime Minister says. Ireland was assured of Common Market membership unofficially by France a few years ago, but it is too closely tied commercially and monetarily with Great Britain to go into the Common Market without the British. (One of Ireland's main attractions as an industrial site is the exemption from customs duties that Britain gives to almost all Irish-made goods.) General de Gaulle's barring of Britain fron the Common Market in 1963 was a sad blow to Lemass.

The slightest suggestion of a completely free trading agreement with other Western European countries would have horrified most Irish businessmen a few years ago, and it still worries a great many of them. But Lemass is confident that the give and take of competition is just the spur that Ireland needs.

AS Northern Ireland faces the last half of the 20th century, it also grapples with an unemployment problem that makes it compete for new industry—but for entirely different reasons. Both shipbuilding, the backbone of Belfast's industrial economy for the past 100 years, and the famed Ulster linen trade are declining. The Northern Irish need jobs in other lines of manufacturing to take up the slack. They envy Lemass's ability to offer enticing grants and tax benefits to foreign investors.

"That's the great advantage of having your own Government," an official in Belfast says. "We can't barter because we haven't got the authority to do so."

A provocative question, discussed with relish in Dublin pubs, is what will happen to Ireland's partition if North and South end up as fellow members of the Common Market. Inevitably, the economies of the two regions will become increasingly interrelated. If that happens, some members of the Government argue, the partition will not last long.

ALL this talk of future economic development and Common Market membership disturbs many people, foreigners as well as Irish, who hate the thought of Ireland's leisurely charm and lovely old castles and cottages giving way to the hustle, noise, six-lane motorways and rectangular buildings of glass and concrete that seem to accompany the arrival of prosperity in every advancing modern country. An elderly Philadelphian gave voice to such fears a while ago while paying a visit to the 12th-century chapel on the Rock of Cashel.

"I haven't a drop of Irish blood in me, but this is my 14th trip to Ireland," he said. "All the other countries in Western Europe—England, France, Germany and Italy—are getting to look like New Jersey. I hope to God they don't spoil Ireland too, at least not for a few more years. Did you read the speech President Kennedy made in the Irish Parliament when he visited Dublin? He said Ireland was never a rich or powerful country, yet since earliest times its influence on the world has been rich and powerful. I didn't always agree with Kennedy, but that's one time he was right. Now, if you'll excuse me I must go and get a glass of Guinness at a nice little pub I found this morning."

It will be many more years before Ireland's charm and ancient beauty is seriously endangered by the rush of progress. But after seven centuries of persecution and then four decades of groping as a free but lonely and often despondent nation, Ireland is happy to be finding its place in the world and knowing, at last, where it is going.

FOR FURTHER READING

CHAPTER 1: IN ISLAND ISOLATION

Behan, Brendan, *Brendan Behan's Island; An Irish Sketch-book*. Hutchinson, 1962.

Creed, Virginia, *All About Ireland*. Duell, Sloan & Pearce, New York, 1951.

Freeman, Thomas Walter, *Ireland: A General and Regional Geography*. Methuen, 1960.

Gorman, Michael, ed., *Ireland by the Irish*. Galley Press, 1963.

Killanin, Lord, and Michael V. Duignan, *Shell Guide to Ireland*. Ebury Press, 1962.

O'Connor, Frank, ed., *A Book of Ireland*. Collins, 1959. *Leinster, Munster and Connaught*. Robert Hale, 1950.

Ryan, A. P., *Islands Apart*. William Morrow, New York, 1954.

Waldron, John, *Ireland*. James Duffy, Dublin, 1958.

CHAPTER 2: THE PEOPLE

Arensberg, Conrad, M., *The Irish Countryman*. Macmillan, 1937.

Beckett, James Camlin, *A Short History of Ireland*. Hutchinson, 1952.

Doyle, Lynn, *The Spirit of Ireland*. Batsford, 1935.

MacManus, Seamas, *The Story of the Irish Race*. Devin-Adair, New York, 1945.

Potter, George W., *To the Golden Door; The Story of the Irish in Ireland and America*. Little, Brown, Boston, Mass., 1960.

Robertson, Olivia, *It's an Old Irish Custom*. Dennis Dobson, 1953.

CHAPTER 3: THE BITTER YEARS

Curtis, Edmund, *A History of Ireland*. Methuen, 1964. *A History of Medieval Ireland from 1100 to 1513*. Methuen, 1938.

Curtis, L. P. Jr., *Coercion and Conciliation in Ireland, 1880-1892*. Princeton University Press, 1963.

Ireland, Tom, *Ireland, Past and Present*. G. P. Putnam's Sons, New York, 1942.

Joyce, P. W., *A Social History of Ancient Ireland*. Longmans, 1963.

O'Faolain, Sean, *King of the Beggars; A Life of Daniel O'Connell*. Nelson, 1938.

O'Siochain, P. A., *Aran, Islands of Legend*. Foilsiúcháin Eireann, Dublin, 1962.

Powell, Thomas G. E., *The Celts*. Thames & Hudson, 1959.

Raftery, Joseph, *Prehistoric Ireland*. Batsford, 1951.

Woodham-Smith, Cecil, *The Great Hunger*. Hamish Hamilton, 1962.

CHAPTER 4: THE TROUBLES

Bennett, Richard L., *The Black and Tans*. Edward Hulton, 1959.

Brennan, Robert, *Allegiance*. Browne & Nolan, Dublin, 1950.

Bromage, Mary C., *De Valera and the March of a Nation*. Hutchinson, 1956.

Caulfield, Max, *The Easter Rebellion*. Muller, 1964.

Colum, Padraic, *Arthur Griffith*. Browne & Nolan, Dublin, 1959.

Fox, Richard Michael, *The History of the Irish Citizen Army*. James Duffy, Dublin, 1943.

Gleeson, James, *Bloody Sunday*. Peter Davies, 1962.

Gwynn, Denis, *De Valera*. Jarrolds, 1933. *The Life and Death of Roger Casement*. Jonathan Cape, 1930.

Horgan, John J., *Parnell to Pearse*. Browne & Nolan, Dublin, 1948.

Macardle, Dorothy, *The Irish Republic*. Gollancz, 1937.

Macmanus, M. J., *Eamon de Valera*. Talbot Press, Dublin, 1962.

CHAPTER 5: THE CHURCH

Bieler, Ludwig, *Ireland: Harbinger of the Middle Ages*. Oxford University Press, 1963. *The Life and Legend of St. Patrick*. Burns, Oates & Washbourne, 1949.

De Paor, Maire and Liam, *Early Christian Ireland*. Thames & Hudson, 1958

Moore, Henry K., *Ireland and Her Church*. W. Tempest, Dundalk, 1937.

Mould, D. D. C. P., *Ireland of the Saints*. Batsford, 1953.

O'Faolain, Sean, *The Irish*. Penguin Books, 1947.

CHAPTER 6: LITERATURE AND THE ARTS

Barnet, Sylvan, and others, eds., *The Genius of the Irish Theater*. Mentor Books, New York, 1960.

Boyd, Ernest, *Ireland's Literary Renaissance*. Grant Richards, 1923.

Carney, James, *Studies in Irish Literature and History*. Dublin Institute for Advanced Studies, 1955.

Colum, Mary Gunning and Padraic, *Our Friend James Joyce*. Gollancz, 1959.

Colum, Padraic, ed., *Treasury of Irish Folklore*. Crown Publishers, New York, 1954.

Corkery, Daniel, *The Hidden Ireland*. M. H. Gill & Son, Dublin, 1956.

Curtayne, Alice, *The Irish Story*. Burns & Oates, 1962.

Dillon, Myles, *Early Irish Literature*. University of Chicago Press, 1948.

Eglinton, John, *Irish Literary Portraits*. Macmillan, 1935.

Howarth, Herbert, *Irish Writers, 1880-1940*. Rockliff, 1958. *Irish Writers, Literature, Under Parnell's Star*. Hill & Wang, New York, 1958.

Hyde, Douglas, *The Story of Gaelic Literature*. Talbot Press, Dublin, 1938.

Garrity, Devin, ed., *44 Irish Short Stories; An Anthology of Irish Short Fiction from Yeats to Frank O'Connor*. Devin-Adair, New York, 1955. *The Irish Genius*. Mentor Books, New York, 1960.

Gwynn, Stephen, *Irish Literature and Drama in the English Language*. Nelson, 1936.

Henry, Françoise, *Irish Art in the Early Period*. Methuen, 1940.

Hoagland, Kathleen, ed., *1,000 Years of Irish Poetry*. Devin-Adair, New York, 1947.

Jeffares, A. Norman, *W. B. Yeats: Man and Poet*. Routledge & Kegan Paul, 1949.

Joyce, Stanislaus, *My Brother's Keeper; James Joyce's Early Years*. Faber & Faber, 1958.

Leask, Harold G., *Irish Castles and Castellated Houses*. W. Tempest, Dundalk, 1941. *Irish Churches and Monastic Buildings*. 3 vols. Dundalgan Press, Dundalk, 1955-1960.

MacDonagh, Donagh, and Lennox Robinson, eds., *The Oxford Book of Irish Verse, 17th-20th Century*. Oxford University Press, 1958.

MacManus, Seumas, *Hibernian Nights*. Macmillan, New York, 1963.

Mercier, Vivian, and David H. Greene, eds., *1,000 Years of Irish Prose*. Universal Library, New York, 1961.

O'Connor, Frank, ed., *Modern Irish Short Stories*. Oxford University Press, 1957.

O'Sullivan, Donal, ed., *Songs of the Irish; An Anthology of Irish Folk Music and Poetry with English Verse Translations*. Browne & Nolan, Dublin, 1960.

Robinson, Lennox, *Ireland's Abbey Theatre*. Sidgwick & Jackson, 1951.

Simpson, Alan, *Beckett and Behan and a Theatre in Dublin*. Routledge & Kegan Paul, 1962.

Tindall, William York, *A Reader's Guide to James Joyce*. Thames & Hudson, 1959. *James Joyce*. Evergreen Books, 1960.

Yeats, W. B., *Collected Poems*. 2nd ed. Macmillan, 1950.

Chapter 7: Northern Ireland

Carson, William A., *Ulster and the Irish Republic*. William W. Cleland, Belfast, 1956

Gallagher, Frank, *The Indivisible Ireland*. Gollancz, 1959.

Gywnn, Denis, *The History of Partition*. Browne & Nolan, Dublin, 1950.

O'Hegarty, Patrick S., *A History of Ireland under the Union*. Methuen, 1952.

Pakenham, Frank, *Peace by Ordeal*. Jonathan Cape, 1935.

Shearman, Hugh, *Ulster*. Robert Hale, 1949.

Ulster since 1800. Twelve Talks Broadcast in the Northern Ireland Home Service of the B.B.C. British Broadcasting Corporation, 1955.

Wilson, Thomas, ed., *Ulster under Home Rule*. Oxford University Press, 1955.

Chapters 8 and 9: Rural and Urban Life

Arensberg, Conrad M., and Solon T. Kimball, *Family and Community in Ireland*. Harvard University Press, 1940.

Behan, Dominic, *Teems of Times and Happy Returns*. Heinemann, 1961.

Joyce, James, *Dubliners*. Penguin Books.

Synge, John Millington, *The Aran Islands*. Allen & Unwin, 1961.

Chapter 10: The Future

Briscoe, Robert, and Alden Hatch, *For the Life of Me*. Longmans, Green, 1959.

McCracken, J. L., *Representative Government in Ireland*. Oxford University Press, 1958.

O'Brien, C. C., ed., *The Shaping of Modern Ireland*. Routledge & Kegan Paul, 1960.

FAMOUS IRISH CULTURAL FIGURES AND THEIR PRINCIPAL WORKS

Literature

Keating, Geoffrey	c.1570-1646	History of Ireland in Gaelic: *Forus Feasa ar Eirinn*. Poetry
Broder, David (Daibhidh O'Bruadair)	c.1625-c.1698	Poetry in Gaelic
Swift, Jonathan	1667-1745	Satires: *Gulliver's Travels, A Tale of a Tub, A Modest Proposal*
O'Rahilly, Egan (Aodhagan O'Rathaille)	c.1670-1726	Gaelic poetry decrying the ruin of Ireland
Farquhar, George	1678-1707	Plays: *The Recruiting Officer, The Beaux' Stratagem*
Berkeley, George	1685-1753	Philosophy: *New Theory of Vision, Dialogues, Treatise concerning the Principles of Human Knowledge*
Burke, Edmund	1729-1797	Political philosophy: *Vindication of Natural Society, Reflections on the Revolution in France*
Goldsmith, Oliver	c.1730-1774	Novel: *The Vicar of Wakefield*. Play: *She Stoops to Conquer*. Poetry: *The Deserted Village*. Essays
O'Sullivan, Owen Roe (Eoghan Ruadh O'Suilleabhain)	c.1746-1784	Gaelic poetry
Merriman, Brian	1747-1805	Gaelic poetry: *Cuirt an Mheanoiche (The Midnight Court)*
Sheridan, Richard Brinsley	1751-1816	Plays: *The School for Scandal, The Rivals, The Critic*
Edgeworth, Maria	1767-1849	Novel: *Castle Rackrent*
Moore, Thomas	1779-1852	Poetry: *Irish Melodies*, including "Believe Me, If All Those Endearing Young Charms", "The Harp That Once through Tara's Halls"
Raftery, Anthony	1784-1835	Gaelic poetry
Mangan, James Clarence	1803-1849	Poetry: "Dark Rosaleen"
LeFanu, Joseph Sheridan	1814-1873	Ghost stories: *In a Glass Darkly*. Novel: *Uncle Silas*
O'Grady, Standish James	1846-1928	Epic history of Ireland: *Heroic Period, Cuchulain and His Contemporaries*
Lady Gregory, Isabella Augusta	1852-1932	Patron of the Irish literary revival. Wrote plays for the Abbey Theatre

154

Moore, George	1852-1933	Novels: *Esther Waters, The Lake, A Drama in Muslin.* Memoirs: *Confessions of a Young Man, Hail and Farewell*
Wilde, Oscar	1854-1900	Plays: *The Importance of Being Earnest, Lady Windermere's Fan.* Poetry: *The Ballad of Reading Gaol.* Novel: *The Picture of Dorian Gray.* Criticism: *Intentions*
Shaw, George Bernard	1856-1950	Plays: *Candida, Caesar and Cleopatra, Man and Superman, John Bull's Other Island, Pygmalion, Saint Joan, Heartbreak House*
Martyn, Edward	1859-1923	Play: *The Heather Field*
Hyde, Douglas	1860-1949	Literary history: *A Literary History of Ireland.* Wrote original poetry and translated into English such Gaelic poems as *Love Songs of Connacht*
Yeats, William Butler	1865-1939	Founder of the Irish literary revival and a moving force in the Abbey Theatre. Poetry: "Sailing to Byzantium", "Among School Children", "Easter 1916", "A Prayer for My Daughter", "Under Ben Bulben". Plays: *The Countess Cathleen, Cathleen ni Houlihan, Deirdre.* Autobiography, essays
Æ (George William Russell)	1867-1935	Poetry, essays
Synge, John Millington	1871-1909	Plays: *The Playboy of the Western World, Riders to the Sea, In the Shadow of the Glen, The Tinker's Wedding, The Well of the Saints*
Corkery, Daniel	1878-	Literary history and criticism
Gogarty, Oliver St. John	1878-1957	Memoirs: *As I Was Going Down Sackville Street, It Isn't This Time of Year at All.* Poetry
Lord Dunsany, Edward John Moreton Drax Plunkett	1878-1957	Plays, novels, short stories, memoirs, poetry
O'Casey, Sean	1880-1964	Plays: *The Shadow of a Gunman, Juno and the Paycock, The Plough and the Stars.* Autobiography
Column, Padraic	1881-	Poetry: *Wild Earth.* Plays, stories, novels, essays
Joyce, James	1882-1941	Novels: *A Portrait of the Artist as a Young Man, Ulysses, Finnegans Wake.* Short stories: *Dubliners.* Play: *Exiles.* Poetry: *Chamber Music*
Stephens, James	1882-1950	Fantasy: *The Crock of Gold.* Poetry
Clarke, Austin	1896-	Poetry
O'Flaherty, Liam	1897-	Novels: *The Informer, Skerret, Famine.* Short stories
Bowen, Elizabeth	1899-	Novels: *The Death of the Heart, A World of Love, The Little Girls.* Short stories
Carroll, Paul Vincent	1900-	Plays: *Shadow and Substance, The White Steed*
O'Faolain, Sean	1900-	Biographies of famous Irish men and women: Daniel O'Connell, Countess Markievicz, Eamon de Valera. Novels, stories, essays
O'Connor, Frank (Michael O'Donovan)	1903-1966	Short stories: *Guest of the Nation, Bones of Contention, Crab Apple Jelly, Traveller's Samples, Domestic Relations.* Novels: *The Saint and Mary Kate, Dutch Interior.* Criticism: *The Mirror in the Roadway*
Beckett, Samuel	1906-	Plays: *Waiting for Godot, Endgame, Happy Days.* Novels: *Murphy, Watt,* the *Molloy* trilogy, *How It Is*
Murdoch, Iris	1919-	Novels: *A Severed Head, Under the Net, The Unicorn, The Italian Girl*
Moore, Brian	1921-	Novels: *The Lonely Passion of Judith Hearne, The Luck of Ginger Coffey, An Answer From Limbo*
Behan, Brendan	1923-1964	Plays: *The Quare Fellow, The Hostage.* Autobiography: *Borstal Boy*
Leonard, Hugh (John Keys Byrne)	1926-	Play: *Stephen D.*
O'Brien, Edna	1932-	Novels: *The Country Girls, August is a Wicked Month*

ART AND ARCHITECTURE

Hone, Nathaniel I	1717-1784	Portrait paintings and engravings
Smyth, Edward	1749-1812	Sculpture: statues for Dublin's Custom House
Johnston, Francis	1761-1829	Architecture: St. George's Church and the General Post Office in Dublin
Kirk, Thomas	1777-1845	Sculpture: did the statue of Lord Nelson on top of the demolished Dublin memorial
Hogan, John	1800-1858	Sculpture: statue of the *Dead Christ* in St. Teresa's Church in Dublin
Woodward, Benjamin	1815-1861	Architecture: the Museum Buildings at Trinity College in Dublin
Foley, John Henry	1818-1874	Sculpture: numerous statues, including figures for the Prince Albert memorial in London and one of Stonewall Jackson in Richmond, Virginia. He also designed the seal of the Confederacy
Hone, Nathaniel II	1831-1917	Painting: land- and seascapes
Yeats, John Butler	1839-1922	Portrait paintings. Father of William Butler Yeats
Orpen, William	1870-1931	Painting: portraits and scenes from Irish life
Yeats, Jack Butler	1871-1957	Painting: impressionistic oils with Irish themes, particularly of circuses, prize-fights and horses
Healy, Michael	1873-1941	Stained-glass windows
Keating, Sean	1889-	Paintings: portraits and Aran Island landscapes
Hone, Evie	1894-1955	Stained-glass windows, notably the Crucifixion window in Eton's war-damaged 15th-century chapel
Jellett, Mainie	1897-1944	Stained-glass windows and religious paintings
O'Sullivan, Sean	1906-	Portraits of William Butler Yeats and others
Scott, Michael	1906-	Architecture: Dublin's central bus terminal, TV centre and other modern structures
Murphy, Seamus	1907-	Sculpture: bust of Countess Markievicz and a memorial to the Fenian leader, Jeremiah O'Donovan Rossa, in Dublin
Collins, Patrick	1911-	Misty landscape paintings
LeBrocquy, Louis	1916-	Abstract landscape paintings and boldly colourful fabric designs
Scott, Patrick	1921-	Abstract paintings

Credits

The sources for the illustrations in this book appear below. Credits for pictures from left to right are separated by commas, from top to bottom by dashes.

Cover—Brian Seed
8, 9—Brian Seed
13—drawings by Adolph E. Brotman
17 to 21—Brian Seed
22, 23—Brian Seed, Farrell Grehan
24—Farrell Grehan
29—map by Rafael D. Palacios
33 to 37—Brian Seed
38, 39—Brian Seed except bottom left and right; Farrell Grehan
40 to 43—Brian Seed
47—map by Enrico Arno
52, 53—Brian Seed
54—Heinz Zinram for TIME
55—Rex Roberts courtesy National Museum of Ireland—Research Laboratory, British Museum courtesy National Museum of Ireland
56—Brian Seed

57—Radio Times Hulton Picture Library
58, 59—Radio Times Hulton Picture Library except left; Culver Pictures top right; Brown Brothers
60, 61—Radio Times Hulton Picture Library
69—Joe Cashman
70, 71—Joe Cashman except right; Central Press—Radio Times Hulton Picture Library
72—P. A. Reuter
73—Radio Times Hulton Picture Library—Carl Mydans, Brian Seed
74—Brian Seed
80 to 88—Brian Seed
95—Berenice Abbott
96—by Karsh, Ottawa, Culver Pictures—National Gallery of Ireland

97—Gjon Mili—Jerry Bauer
98—Brian Seed—William MacQuitty
99—courtesy Waddington Galleries—Eric Schaal, courtesy New School Art Center
100—Brian Seed
106 to 112—Brian Seed
119, 120—Brian Seed
121—Alan Clifton
122 to 125—Brian Seed
126, 127—Derek Bayes for SPORTS ILLUSTRATED
128, 129—Toni Frissell except bottom left; Brian Seed
130—Brian Seed
136 to 140—Brian Seed
141—John Sadovy for TIME
142, 143—John Sadovy for TIME except bottom left; Brian Seed
144—Farrell Grehan
149, 150, 151—Brian Seed

ACKNOWLEDGMENTS

The editors of this volume are indebted to the following: William Y. Tindall, Professor of English, Columbia University, New York; the Reverend Sean Corkery, Librarian, St. Patrick's College, Maynooth, Ireland; and J. G. Simms, Assistant to the Professor of Modern History, Trinity College, Dublin. Valuable assistance was also provided by Juan M. Greene, Council Member and former President of the Irish National Farmers' Association, Jack Loudan of Belfast, Maureen Snowball Green of London and John Nagle of New York.

Index

This symbol in front of a page numbers indicates a photograph or painting of the subject mentioned.